I Promise to Hate, Despise, and Abuse You until Death Do Us Part

Marriage in a Narcissistic Age

Andrea V. Oelger
Troy W. Martin

Bookend Publishers
Bourbonnais, Illinois

Bookend Publishers, Inc.
P. O. Box 1351
Bourbonnais, IL 60914
www.bookendpublishers.com

Manufactured in the United States of America

Library of Congress Cataloging-in-Publication Data

Oelger, Andrea V.
I promise to hate, despise, and abuse you until death do us part: marriage in a narcissistic age / Andrea V. Oelger and Troy W. Martin
p. cm.
1. Marriage. 2. Divorce. 3. Narcissism. 4. Church work with abused women 5. Wife abuse—religious aspects—Christianity 6. Wife abuse—United States—psychological aspects 7. Man-woman relationships 8. Interpersonal conflict—United States I. Troy W. Martin II. Title

Cover design by Robert Carroll

ISBN 978-0-615-40656-5

Table of Contents

Preface

This book represents the experiences of many, many women who have been recruited to become the wives of narcissists. The extent of their suffering is beyond description. Nevertheless, this book gives some of them a voice as they speak out about the abusive treatment they have endured at the hands of their narcissistic husbands.

Many of the stories in this book arise out of lived experiences and are factually based. They are drawn from several years of ministerial and professional experience. However, the persons described in this book are composite characters, and many readers will probably see themselves in one or another of these stories because, sadly, these stories depict events and situations that happen all too often in our society. Narcissism is on the rise and so are the suffering and toxicity it brings to marriages.[1]

This book offers insights to these women that will enable them to understand what they are really up against in their marriages, but it also offers hope by removing many misguided

---

[1] Jean M. Twenge and W. Keith Campbell, *The Narcissism Epidemic: Living in the Age of Entitlement* (New York: Free Press, 2009). See also Jean M. Twenge, *Generation Me: Why Today's Young Americans Are More Confident, Assertive, Entitled—and More Miserable Than Ever Before* (New York: Free Press, 2006).

notions that keep these women trapped in these toxic marriages. It investigates the Bible's influence on society in promoting male domination and female subordination as well as the church's prohibition against divorce. This book presents new insights to show that the Bible actually permits a wife to leave her narcissistic husband and to seek a divorce. If a wife decides to remain with him, however, this book discusses essential strategies she'll need for her survival.

This book is thus intended to be helpful to these women, and for this reason, it is intentionally short and simple. Women in these toxic marriages usually have little time or energy left to wade through a thick, dense book. Many of these women will be able to read this book with little effort in a few hours, but it will take much longer for them to perfect the strategies of dealing with their narcissistic husbands and ex-husbands, and they may need to refer back to the book many times. They may also need to consult other books and professionals services that provide more specific psychological, relational, and legal information.

The ideas in this book have been presented publicly on several occasions, and the authors would like to thank Solocon Midwest in Roach, MO; Solocon East in Middletown, MD; Solocon Canada in Olds, Canada; Rev. Gary Reiss and the Grand Haven Church of the Nazarene in Grand Haven, MI; Kendra Testerman and the Mothers of Preschool Children at the Manteno Church of the Nazarene in Manteno, IL; and the Adult

Sunday School Class at Trinity Evangelical Covenant Church in Chicago, IL. The encouraging and helpful comments we received from those in attendance at these events have provided much assistance to us in the writing of this book.

We would also like to express our gratitude to those who read copies of our manuscript and offered their comments and suggestions. In particular, we would like to thank Sheryl Martin, Amie Weethee, Janice Smith, Mary Ellen Couch, Marilue Bryant, Rev. Tom and Lauralee Nothstein, Rev. Kendall Franklin, and Prof. Avis Clendenen. The published version of this book is much improved because of their comments and contributions.

Most of all, our hearts go out to all those women who are trapped in toxic marriages with narcissistic husbands. We have heard your silent suffering, and we have seen your invisible wounds. We hope that our book will give you some insight or some strategy that will help you when you feel your situation is beyond hope. We trust our book will be a key that unlocks the door of your torture chamber so you can be free.

Andrea V. Oelger
Troy W. Martin

Introduction

A Father's Story

She looked so beautiful dressed in her pure, white wedding gown as we stood in a small room to wait for the wedding coordinator to tell us it was time for her to make her grand entry. She was my precious daughter whom I loved more than life itself. I knew we'd never share this unique moment again, and I wanted to say just the right thing to her.

When I opened my mouth, I was surprised to hear these words come out, "Are you sure you want to do this? If you tell me that you don't want to go through with this, I'll march to the front of the church and announce that a huge mistake has been avoided today and that there will be no marriage. I'll invite everyone to go to the reception and enjoy the meal that has been prepared and celebrate the avoidance of this mistake."

What had I just said? I couldn't believe it. This was her wedding day. How could I risk spoiling it by asking her such a stupid, inappropriate question? I could tell she was somewhat taken off-guard by my question but nevertheless reassured me, "It'll be okay, dad."

I silently thought about what prompted me to ask such an inappropriate question on what was supposed to be the happiest day of her life. I'd not been thrilled when my daughter started dating him. She was so talented and gifted; he talked a good game but never really achieved anything. My daughter sailed through college in less than four years with outstanding grades; he'd wanted to be an electrical engineer but couldn't pass some of the classes, and so he took a liberal studies degree.

My daughter was so nice and considerate of everyone; he was abrasive, and I found myself always on my guard when I was around him. My daughter was kind and giving; he was selfish and a taker.

I worried about her and hoped she'd see through him and end the relationship before marrying him. I even tried to explain his personality to her and paid for them to receive pre-marital counseling. None of my efforts succeeded.

I wanted to say "No" when he came to ask for her hand in marriage, but as I looked into my daughter's joy-filled eyes, I couldn't bring myself to dash her happiness at that moment. So, how could I risk bringing sadness to her wedding day?

My thoughts were interrupted by a knock on the door, and we walked arm-in-arm down the aisle to the front of the church. One of the most conflicted moments of my life was when the minister asked, "Who gives this woman to be married to this man?"

This woman was not just any woman. She was my daughter. How could I give her to someone whom I suspected would not love and care for her as I did? How could I give her to someone whom I did not trust to honor and respect her as I did? How could I give her to someone whom I was convinced would not cherish and treasure her as I did? How could I?

But I did and managed to answer, “Her mother and I.” I placed her hand in his just as I’d been instructed by the wedding coordinator and took my seat next to my wife. I have no words to describe how horrible I felt at that very moment.

During the next few years, I saw my daughter only on special occasions such as birthdays and holidays. I wanted to ask her how her marriage was going and how she was doing, but I didn’t want to pry. I feared something was really wrong, but the only indication I had was a comment she made one day as she left my house. Just before she walked out the door, she looked at me and said, “Dad, you’re the wisest man I know.”

I didn’t quite know how to respond, for her comment was in stark contrast to her assessment of me throughout her teenage years. I wondered if my sudden increase in wisdom might not be due to her realization that I’d been right about him, but I couldn’t be sure.

I was sure, however, when she showed up at my home one day and asked if she could stay. I said, “Well, yes. You’re always welcome here. You’re my daughter.”

She continued, “Dad, something is wrong, and I don’t know what it is.”

My daughter is a very intelligent girl, and I was surprised that she couldn’t even begin to describe what was wrong so I asked, “What do you think it might be? Do you have a clue?”

"I don't know, dad, but something is really wrong. I'm a horrible wife and mother, and I can't stand myself."

Her words baffled me. She was a wonderful mother and a giving wife. Everyone loved to be around her. She was so kind-hearted and generous in sharing her time and energies with others. I didn't really know how to respond but finally said, "I don't agree with how you see yourself, but if you feel something is wrong, I'm here for you and I'll help you find out what it is, if we can."

Over the next few days, I cleared my schedule and we talked and talked. We surfed the internet and read books about relationships as we struggled to wrap our minds around her problem. We were floundering around in a fog until we found an article on the internet by Amy Wildman White that presented a case study of a toxic narcissistic relationship.[1] After we read about that wife's impossible struggle with a narcissistic husband, my daughter said, "Dad, you can replace that woman's name with mine and her husband's name with my husband's name, and you'll have an almost exact description of my marriage."

I was shocked. Had my daughter really endured such unimaginable horrors? Had she really been so intimidated, put

---

[1] Amy Wildman White, "The Silent Killer of Christian Marriages," Chapter 7 in *Healing the Hurting: Giving Hope and Help to Abused Women* (Catherine Clark Kroeger and James R. Beck, eds.; Grand Rapids: Baker, 1998), 99-108.

down, criticized, humiliated, and threatened? Had she actually been forced to live in denial of her feelings and to dissociate herself from her experiences just to survive?

She had entered marriage with such high hopes and dreams. Had her dreams become a nightmare filled with fear, terror, helplessness, self-contempt, and shame, a nightmare from which she felt there was no waking up or escape for her? I could hardly stand the thought, but at least now we had a handle on her problem.

She and I both realized that she'd been duped, that this person whom she saw during courtship only revealed his oppressive and controlling personality after snagging her for his wife. The warning signs were there, but she just couldn't see them.

During the next few weeks, we read every book about narcissism we could find. As we read, she'd say, "So that is why he'd say these things to me." As we read, she'd say, "So that explains why he'd do the things he did." As we read, she'd say, "So that's the reason he'd treat me the way he did."

As we discovered more and more, her self-understanding grew and grew until one day she asked me, "Dad, I know you don't approve of divorce, but would you go with me to see a divorce lawyer?"

She was right. I didn't approve of divorce, but the knowledge I'd gained about her situation and the horrors she'd endured made me question my view of divorce. I'd reached the conclusion that she had no good options and that divorce was probably the most preferable of the bad ones. So, I answered her, "Sure, you know I will."

The lawyer listened to us and agreed to file the papers and then said to my daughter, "There is one problem. You can't stay with your dad. You must return to your own home or risk losing your children."

In panic, I raised my voice to the lawyer, "She can't," I said gasping, "Her home is a torture chamber."

"She must," he said, "or be viewed as abandoning her children."

Grasping for any other way, I said, "Well, can't we just bring her children over to my house?"

He firmly responded, "You've no legal authorization, and the court will not look favorably on your removing the children from their home."

"Who makes such stupid laws!" I yelled.

"Please don't get upset at me," he said, "I'm only giving you my best legal advice. She must return to her home." Then, he asked my daughter, "Do you think you can do that?"

She thought but only for a brief moment and then said, "I'd do anything for my children."

The next several months were pure hell as we waited on a cruel legal system to take its unjust time to hear her case. She'd call me in the middle of the night, and I could hear him ranting and raging at her in the background.

I'm not a violent man, but if I were ever capable of murder, this was definitely the time. I wanted to rescue my daughter, but I couldn't. I was her dad, and I was supposed to protect her, but an inept legal system tied my hands and blocked my every attempt. I pushed the lawyer, but with no results. I could only stand by helplessly and watch her endure inexpressible abuse from her narcissistic husband.

As I watched her subject herself to such unimaginable horrors for the sake of her children, I felt so much pride in her. She truly was my precious daughter. She was so strong. I don't see how anyone could've survived the abuse she endured during those terrible months, but she did.

A few years later when the broken legal system finally got around to finalizing her divorce, she was awarded sole custody of her children. Her sacrifice had paid off, and her children, my grandchildren, at least have a chance in life because of her. I can't express how proud I am of her.

One day, she asked me, "Dad, do you remember the time when we waited in that small room on my wedding day and you told me you'd march to the front of the church and call off my wedding?"

My anxiety level rose and a fleeting thought crossed my mind that she might blame me for spoiling her wedding day and placing such a doubt in her mind so that her marriage failed. I braced myself and answered, "Yes, I remember. How could I forget?" I started to explain why I'd made that statement, but she quickly cut me off.

She firmly continued, "I knew it was the wrong thing for me to go through with my wedding. During our engagement, I'd already begun to see some of his controlling and abusive behaviors, but I'd gone so far that I didn't think I could turn back at that point. I realize now that turning back at that point would've been so much easier. It scared me a little when you made that statement, dad, because I knew you'd have marched to the front of the church and called off my wedding. I was just too embarrassed for you to do that, but, dad, I'm alive today because you told me you'd do that."

"What do you mean?" I asked.

"I mean that several times in my painful marriage I considered suicide. I could see no other way out of my situation. Believe me, dad, death was preferable to living with my husband. What saved me, dad, was that statement you made in that small room on my wedding day. I knew that if you were willing to humiliate yourself in front of the entire church to protect me that you'd do anything for me, even go through a divorce with me."

Tears of relief filled my eyes. I'd been so haunted by that statement ever since I'd made it because I'd thought it'd caused my daughter pain. What a relief to know that my statement had actually saved her life. I hugged her tightly and said, "I'm so sorry for all you've had to suffer. I wanted to protect you, and I would've marched to the front of that church."

"I know you would've, dad," she said, "but thank you for giving me the opportunity to find out for myself."

I hugged her even more tightly and said, "I love you more than anyone can ever know, and I'd do anything for you. You're my daughter, and I'm your dad forever."

A Guide for Reading this Book

At a most profound moment of human existence, a man and a woman stand at the front of a church and exchange sacred vows promising to love, honor, and cherish each other until death part them. The day is filled with festivities and celebrations, high hopes, expectations, and dreams. According to the fairy tale, they're supposed to live happily ever after.

Sadly, real life isn't a fairy tale, and many marriages end in divorce or worse, a lifetime of misery and pain. High hopes are dashed, expectations frustrated, and dreams shattered. Marriage festivities give way to fights, and nuptial celebrations to conflict and confusion.

What goes wrong with these marriages? While there're perhaps many reasons, a primary cause is narcissism and the narcissistic personality. If one spouse has this personality, the vow is not to love, honor, and cherish but to hate, despise, and abuse the other until death part them, and a toxic marriage is the outcome of such a wedding.

This book is about these toxic marriages caused by narcissism and the narcissistic personality. If your marriage is in trouble and you don't know why, read this book to see if narcissism offers an explanation for your situation. If your marriage has already ended in divorce, read this book to discover if narcissism explains what led to the end of your marriage. If you're not married but are experiencing problems in a relationship in your life, read this book to determine if narcissism is the reason you're experiencing such difficulties.

In Part One of this book, you'll read about the narcissistic personality. See if the characteristics of this personality fit the difficult person in your life. All relationships are complex and take different forms, and some characteristics will fit while others may not. Take what is useful and leave the rest behind.

If this personality fits and you feel trapped in a narcissistic relationship, read Part Two, which describes how male domination and female submission adds to the toxicity of a narcissistic relationship. This second part also explains how the church's stand against divorce preserves toxic narcissistic relationships. The information in this second part will hopefully open the door of your torture chamber and offer you a way out of your toxic relationship.

If you choose to remain in that relationship, however, read Part Three, which provides strategies for surviving a narcissistic relationship.

Narcissism is on the rise in modern American society and so is the suffering caused by narcissistic relationships. Since 1982, thousands of graduating college seniors have completed an evaluation called the Narcissistic Personality Inventory (NPI).[2] For each decade, this inventory indicates that college students are more narcissistic than the decade before. Studies such as the NPI prove that narcissism is indeed spreading in American society. As narcissism increases, the problems caused by narcissistic spouses multiply as well.

Since 75% of all diagnosed cases of the Narcissistic Personality Disorder are men, the majority of narcissistic relationships are caused by a narcissistic male.[3] These relationships are usually far more toxic than those caused by a narcissistic female. Furthermore, over 90% of all domestic abuse is perpetrated by men against their female partners.[4]

---

[2] Jean M. Twenge and W. Keith Campbell, *The Narcissism Epidemic: Living in the Age of Entitlement* (New York: Free Press, 2009). 30-32.

[3] Sam Vaknin, *Malignant Self Love: Narcissism Revisited* (Prague & Skopje: Narcissus Publications, 2003), 21.

[4] This statistic is provided by the New York State Coalition Against Domestic Violence. For additional information, visit the website at http://www.nyscadv.org/domesticviolence.htm.

Therefore, this book is written from the perspective of a female trapped in a toxic relationship with a narcissistic male, and the pronouns for the non-narcissistic partner will be feminine. The primary purpose of this book is to offer freedom and hope to these women.

Statistically of course then, 25% of narcissistic relationships are caused by females, and if you're a male trapped in such a relationship, read this book and reverse the gender designations of the pronouns. This book is not meant to minimize or ignore your experiences. If you're married to a narcissistic wife, you are probably enduring your own private hell, and this book is not meant to minimize or ignore your experiences.

Men, however, are usually better equipped to handle a narcissistic partner than are women. Men are generally physically stronger and do not experience physical threats from a spouse in the same way that a woman does. In the majority of cases, men have jobs and careers that enable them to escape from their narcissistic partners, at least for a time. In these and other ways, men have advantages that enable them to negotiate a narcissistic partner better than many women can. This book, therefore, focuses on women who are generally far more disadvantaged when dealing with a narcissist. Perhaps, a sequel to this book will examine toxic narcissistic relationships from a male victim's perspective, but that book remains to be written.

Part 1

The Recipe for Toxic Marriages: The Narcissistic Ingredients

Chapter 1
A Tragic Story—Old and New

The Narcissistic Personality Disorder was first identified by Heinz Kohut in 1971 and officially recognized by the American Psychiatric Association in 1980, but the disorder and certainly the narcissistic personality has been around probably as long as humans. An old story in the Bible describes a narcissistic personality at work in a marriage relationship in ancient Israel. First, the story from the book of Judges 19:1-30 and then its explanation from a narcissistic perspective.

A Bible Story

This event occurred in those days when there was no king in Israel. A certain Levite man lived in the remote hill country of Ephraim and took for himself a concubine wife from the city of Bethlehem in the territory of Judah.

His concubine became angry with him, and so she left him to return to her father's house in Bethlehem and was there about four months. Her Levite husband finally got up and went after her to speak to her heart and to reconcile with her and to bring her back. He took his servant and a couple of donkeys and came to her father's house.

The girl's father saw him and greeted him joyfully. His father-in-law, the girl's father, made him his guest, and he remained with his father-in-law for three days. They ate and drank and stayed together. On the fourth day, they arose early, and her Levite husband prepared to leave, but her father said to his son-in-law, "Strengthen yourself with some food, and later you may go." Then, the two men sat and ate and drank together once again, and her father implored her husband, "Please spend the night again, and let your heart be merry." When her husband rose to leave, however, her father urged him to stay so he stayed there another night.

On the fifth day, her husband arose early to leave, but her father said, "Strengthen yourself and wait until afternoon." So, the two of them ate once again. When the Levite and his concubine and his servant stood up to leave, her father said to him, "It's now late in the day. Please stay here again all night. The day is ending. Stay here and be merry, and tomorrow you can get up and go home early in the morning."

Her Levite husband refused to spend the night again, however, but stood up and left. He arrived at Jebus, which later is renamed Jerusalem. He had with him a couple of saddled donkeys, and his servant and his concubine were with him. When they arrived at Jebus, it was late in the day, and the servant said to his master, "Let's enter this city of the Jebusites and spend the night there." His master responded to him, "We'll not enter this city of foreigners, who do not belong to the people of the Israelites. No, we'll travel on to Gibeah." Furthermore, he said to his servant, "Let's go and spend the night at Gibeah or at Ramah."

So they continued their journey and went on their way. The sun went down on them near Gibeah, which belongs to the territory of Benjamin, and they entered to spend the night in Gibeah. Her Levite husband sat down in the public square of the city because no one invited them to spend the night in his house. However, an old man was returning at evening from his work in the field. He was from the hill country of Ephraim, but he was living among the Benjamites in Gibeah. This old man looked and saw the traveler in the city square; and this old man asked, "Where are you going and where do you come from?"

The Levite answered him, "We're passing from Bethlehem in Judah to the remote parts of the hill country of Ephraim, where I live. I've been to Bethlehem in Judah, and now I'm returning home. No one has offered us a place to stay. We have straw and feed for our donkeys and bread and wine for us. We're not lacking anything."

The old man replied, "Peace be with you. I'll take care of all your needs, but please don't spend the night in the square." So, the old man brought him into his house and fed the donkeys. They washed their feet and ate and drank.

While they were enjoying themselves, the men of the city surrounded the house, began beating on the door, and said to the old man, "Bring out the traveler who came into your house so that we may have sexual relations with him." The old man went out and said to them, "No, my brothers, don't act so wickedly. This man is my guest. Don't do this evil thing. Inside are my virgin daughter and his concubine. Let me bring them out now. Ravish them and do with them whatever you want, but against this man don't do something so evil." However, the men wouldn't listen to him.

So the Levite seized his concubine and shoved her out to them, and they raped and abused her all during the night until morning. At day break, they let her go. The woman came and collapsed at the door of the old man's house where her Levite master was safely inside. She remained there until full daylight when her Levite master finally woke up.

After he opened the doors of the house and went out to continue his journey, there lay the woman, his concubine, at the door of the house with her hands grasping the threshold. He said to her, "Get up, let's go." There was no answer. Then, he loaded her on his donkey and went home. After he entered his house, he took a knife and dismembered her, limb by limb, into twelve pieces. He then sent a piece of her to each of the territories in the country of Israel.

This tragic story requires explanation. What propels this story forward and leads to the death, dismemberment, and destruction of this nameless woman? What recipe cooked up such a toxic relationship? The answer to these questions is surprisingly simple. Her Levite husband had a narcissistic personality, and narcissism provided the recipe for this toxic relationship. As with all relationships, there are two sides of the story so consideration must be given to the perspective of this woman and her Levite husband and some details must be supplied to explain the gaps in this brief, tragic story.

The story opens with a Levite man choosing a woman as his concubine wife. During the courtship and selection process, she must have felt on top of the world as she exchanged her low self-esteem for his exhilarating praise and worship. He said that he loved just those things that she despised about herself.

She was unaware that narcissists are expert recruiters. When a narcissist is in recruitment mode, the object of his advances can rarely resist. He was out to recruit her into his world so that he could take what he wanted from her. She couldn't have known at this stage that her wants, desires, and wishes meant nothing to him except as recruitment tools to get what he wanted.

So, he won her over and took her away from her father's house in Bethlehem. He moved her far away to his world in the remote hill country of Ephraim. There, she experienced the isolation of social abuse. He took her from her friends and family. His goal was to make her totally dependent on him socially so he could control her. She may have cried, "If only I could visit my folks. If only I had someone to talk to." Her lonely cries only echoed her increasing and eventual total isolation.

In this relationship, she was clearly the inferior. She was his concubine. In the ancient world, a woman who married a man of equal social standing was considered his wife. A woman of lesser social standing was considered a concubine. At first, she felt elation that he, a man of higher social standing, would give her the time of day. During the recruitment stage, he used his higher social standing to make her feel better about herself and to build her up.

After the marriage, however, he constantly placed himself above her and tore her down. He reminded her of her low social standing and how she owed so much to him for even marrying her in the first place. He told her that no one but he could love her with the implication that she was unlovable by anyone else but him.

She experienced the humiliation of emotional abuse.[1] His demeaning words on a daily basis undermined her sense of self-worth. As his inferior, she was there for him and not the other way around. Nothing she did was ever right or worthy of him in his eyes. With his constant barrage of devaluing words, she sank into an emotional abyss filled with feelings of worthlessness.

Since she was a concubine, he was only obligated to provide her with economic support less than that of a wife of equal social standing with him. He controlled the purse strings, and he made it clear to her that she was totally dependent upon him for her food, shelter, and clothing. She had to ask him for everything she needed or wanted and had to express gratitude even for things that were hers by right. Her dismay at the destitution of her economic plight plunged her to despair.

As his mind games became more and more intricate, she felt herself slipping into the madness of psychological abuse. She felt she was going crazy.[2] Although the story does not

---

[1] The notions of emotional abuse, psychological abuse, social abuse, and economic abuse are more fully discussed by Mary Susan Miller, *No Visible Wounds: Identifying Nonphysical Abuse of Women by their Men* (New York: Fawcett Books, 1995), 23-77. See also Beverly Engel, *The Emotionally Abused Woman: Overcoming Destructive Patterns and Reclaiming Yourself* (New York: Fawcett Books, 1990).

[2] George R. Bach and Ronald Deutsch, *Stop! You're Driving Me Crazy* (New York: G. P. Putnam's Sons Publishers, 1980). Bach and Deutsch describe this tactic of the narcissist as "crazy-making."

report until later that he was physically abusive to her, he certainly may have been so all along or at least have threatened her with physical abuse. She may have experienced the trauma of physical abuse and feared he'd kill her as he eventually did.

Many toxic, abusive relationships do not include actual physical abuse but only the threat of it. With such recent national attention on wife-beaters, abusive narcissists are careful not to cross the line but find other, less visible ways to dish out their abuse and establish their control.

Whatever was going on in that home, the relationship was so toxic that she finally mustered the courage to leave him. She returned to her father's house in Bethlehem. Why did she leave?

The story reports that she became angry with him (Revised Standard Version). Other translations of the story assert that she was unfaithful to him (New American Bible) or had an affair with another man (King James Version and New American Standard Bible).[3] In whatever translation you read, she's the one blamed for the breakup of this home. She left.

---

[3] The variations in the translations arise from the ambiguous meaning of the Hebrew verb זנה. This verb can mean to be unfaithful to a husband by having sexual relations with another man. However, it can also mean to be angry with someone. The latter meaning is more probable here because the Septuagint, an old Greek translation of the Hebrew, renders this Hebrew verb by the Greek word for anger. In addition, this woman would probably have been killed in this society as a penalty for her adultery, if indeed she had committed adultery against her husband. See Exodus 20:14; Leviticus 20:10; Deuteronomy 5:18; 22:22.

Her Levite husband could now play the role of the victim and recruit others to give him sympathy for how he was wronged by this woman. She was re-victimized and has been re-victimized ever since by all the translations of this story that blame her for the breakup.

Sadly, the true victim of a toxic narcissistic relationship is usually blamed while the narcissist enjoys the sympathy and support of everyone else. The true victim is bewildered by the ease with which he seduces others for his cause. Narcissists are very good at playing the victim all the while they're dishing out the worst abuses imaginable on their poor, isolated, destitute, defenseless wives. This woman's experience is enough to drive her insane or at least to make her doubt her sanity.

This woman's only fault was that she broke her marriage contract with him to clean, cook, and care for him. She left, and that was her only fault. His faults were far greater than hers. His faults were the cause of her leaving and not being able to take his abuses any longer. Had he made a loving, caring, and supportive home for her, she'd never have left. Had he lived up to his vow to love, honor, and cherish her, she'd have remained with him until the end of her days. His vow to her, however, was to hate, despise, and abuse her, and she finally concluded that leaving was her only option for survival. So, she returned to her father's house in Bethlehem.

Now, her Levite husband waited four months to go after her. He probably thought that four months was enough time to convince her that he didn't need her and that she was worthless to him. Of course, nothing could've been further from the truth.

He needed her far more than she needed him. She could've lived the rest of her days in her father's house, but his need for someone to clean, cook, and look after him eventually drove him to go after her. Narcissists are experts at exchanging a lie for the truth and then making the lie really appear as the truth. He was an expert narcissist.

What happens next is one of the most pathetic parts of this old story. When the Levite arrived at her father's house, her father received him gladly. This father who was charged with the responsibility of protecting his daughter received her narcissistic abuser gladly. Her father should have made it clear to him in no uncertain terms that he was not welcome. Anyone who would treat his daughter with such disregard had no place in his house. Her pathetic father, however, not only received him but also wined and dined him for five days.

The story is very clear. The two of them, the father and his son-in-law, and only the two of them ate and drank. She was left out with the thankless task of serving her father and husband but did not partake with them in their eating and drinking. She'd returned to her father's house for protection, but her father was co-opted by her husband, and her father gave her up to her abuser. A more pathetic character than her father is difficult to find anywhere.

As she left on the fifth day with her abusive husband, how anxious and empty she must have felt. How hopeless her situation must have seemed to her. In her mind, she had few options. She could seek escape in alcoholism to numb the pain she constantly felt, or she could take the drastic option of suicide to escape her hopeless plight.

Many wives of Narcissistic husbands consider or even take these options. What was she thinking? The story does not say but only reports that she traveled on with him firmly in his control. He made the decisions, and she felt she could do nothing but comply.

One decision he made reveals another aspect of his narcissistic personality. As they neared Jebus, his servant suggested that they spend the night there. The Levite refused because the Jebusites were foreigners, not Israelites. The Levite felt superior to the Jebusites and refused to associate with them. Narcissists often have feelings of superiority and refuse to associate with those whom they consider inferior. This Levite exhibited this narcissistic character trait, and so they traveled to Gibeah, where this Levite thought those worthy of his company resided.

Whatever this Levite may have thought about the residents of Gibeah, they were not at all welcoming to him. Only an old man who was not a native resident of Gibeah took him in along with his concubine and servant. That night, she experienced the only character in the story that treated her kindly. He washed her feet and included her in the meal along with her husband. His kindness, however, was short-lived.

When the men of the city besieged the house and demanded that the old man send out the Levite so that they could sexually assault him, the old man offered to send out his daughter and the Levite's concubine.

Did she hear him correctly? Had he offered to send her out to that sex-crazed mob? Before she could comprehend what was happening, her Levite husband shoved her out the door to face that mob alone. He was supposed to be her protector, but he turned her over to that mob to protect himself. She was dispensable and unimportant in his estimation. Only he and his needs merited consideration.

The mob sexually assaulted and abused her until the morning when it let her go. She struggled to the door and grabbed the threshold as she attempted to regain a place of safety, but she collapsed.

Her Levite husband is now called her master. He awakened after a good night's sleep and opened the door to go on his way. He was the master and she was of less worth to him than a slave since he pushed her out instead of his slave who was with him.

As brutal as was his pushing her out to the mob the night before, his treatment of her in the morning was even more insensitive. Instead of going to her and seeing how she was, he commanded her, "Get up, let's go." He had no sympathy or empathy for her or her ordeal. Only his well-being was important. He couldn't even feel empathy for what she had suffered. His lack of empathy was yet one more characteristic of his narcissistic personality.

He commanded her, but she couldn't answer. His abusive treatment of her had silenced her voice forever. He'd completely used her up for his own needs. She had nothing left to give to him, or did she?

He loaded her on his donkey as he would a sack of flour or a stack of firewood. He carried her to his home, took a knife, cut her up into twelve pieces and sent a piece of her to each of the territories of Israel to announce the challenge to his honor at Gibeah. Even in her death, he found a way to use her for his needs, and she has no grave or resting place in Israel. He'd completely and totally used her up.

Narcissists are users. They use everyone around them to meet their own needs. Everyone else is expendable for what the narcissist needs. This narcissistic Levite provided the recipe for this toxic relationship that eventually consumed the life of this poor, unnamed woman who was unfortunately recruited into his narcissistic world. Her name is never spoken and her voice is never heard even once in this story.

In this way, this sad and tragic old story comes to a horrific end. This old story is tragic enough in its own right, but what makes it even more tragic is that this old story is ever new and is played out over and over again. The tragic experience of this unnamed woman is lived out again and again in the lives of too many women in the modern world.

A Stranger's Story

A few years ago as I traveled home late one Sunday afternoon, I was driving through the country, and as I approached a "T" in the road, I saw a rattle-trap blue Chevrolet Cavalier turn the corner and come to a screeching stop in a cloud of dust. I saw a bundle ejected from the passenger door, and the car sped away. As I pulled off to the side of the road, I saw a thin, haggard woman in a tattered dress as she walked barefoot in the direction in which that car had sped away.

I parked and walked up to the woman who was crying and muttering something I couldn't make out. Not sure of what to do, I offered to drive her to a police station or anywhere she wanted to go. She acted as though she didn't hear me and kept walking and crying and muttering. As I contemplated what to do next, that old rattle-trap car came speeding back over the hill, made a u-turn just in front of us, and came to a stop beside the road.

A man stepped out of the car and began to yell at her in an angry voice, "Get in this car immediately." She cowered and limped toward the passenger's door.

Wanting to say something but not knowing what, I said to the man, "You should speak to her more kindly."

He whirled on me and shouted, "She's crazy and deserves everything she gets." I thought to myself that if she were crazy, he'd probably made her that way.

Still wanting to do something to make the situation better for her, I followed him back to his car. After he got into his car, I looked in the backseat and saw three children with terror written all over their faces. I understood then why she kept walking in the direction of that car and why she re-entered that torture chamber. Her children were there.

As that old car raced away for the last time, I was left standing by the side of the road with a flood of emotions rushing through the core of my being. I'd just met that Levite from the old story in Judges, and he was alive and well in the twenty-first century.

I determined right then and there to do something about the plight of women such as the one I'd met by the side of the road that Sunday afternoon. I determined that I'd do everything in my power to free women from the clutches of such narcissistic men, so that this old story wouldn't be ever new.

This book is an attempt to make good on that determination to expose narcissism and its toxic recipe and to allow women trapped in the torture chambers of toxic narcissistic relationships to speak and to find their voices and to reclaim their lives.

Chapter 2
Narcissism Unmasked

In a popular movie entitled *The Mask*, Jim Carey plays a character named Stanley Ipkiss, who is weak, disorganized, unsure of himself, ineffective, and timid until he puts on a magical mask that turns him into a narcissist. When the mask is on, Carey is full of himself, powerful, irresistible, and above the law. The mask hides Carey's genuine character, and he's only truly himself when he removes the mask.[1]

A narcissist is a grandiose actor constantly projecting an image of illusion. The mask portrays confidence, strength, and maturity. A narcissist will say or do anything in any situation to maintain his act. As a matter of fact, he directs all his energies not toward true accomplishments but toward preserving his projected illusion.

He can be exhilarating and exciting when he needs to be. When he's recruiting others to do his bidding, he's irresistibly appealing and charming. Sometimes, he's funny, serious, witty, sad, hurt, and the list goes on. Whatever others need to be recruited, he can act the part so well that they usually offer little

---

[1] Carey's character is developed by a particular understanding of narcissism as a mask for low self-esteem. Jean M. Twenge and W. Keith Campbell (*The Narcissism Epidemic: Living in the Age of Entitlement* [New York: Free Press, 2009], 24-28) challenge this view and propose that overly inflated self-esteem is actually more characteristic of the narcissist.

resistance to becoming supporting actors in his all-about-me movie.

The reality of the narcissist's character is far different, however, from the charming and confident image he projects. In reality, he's a spoiled, selfish, self-centered, undisciplined, unprincipled toddler trapped in an adult's body. He assumes many different roles.[2]

The elitist narcissist relentlessly pursues others that he thinks can help him get ahead, but he really cares nothing for them. He promotes himself and exaggerates his accomplishments and abilities. His self-promotion often results in his attaining positions of power, authority, and prestige for which his relational skills are ill-equipped to handle. The elitist narcissist cultivates special status and recognition and by his illusory success frustrates others that are truly making significant contributions.

The amorous narcissist deceptively projects an intense desire for close, intimate relationships but is really only interested in exploiting another's body for his own pleasure and to satisfy his own appetites. He really cares nothing for anyone else.

---

[2] For the various types, see T. Millon, R. Davis, C. Millon, L. Escovar, and S. Meagher, *Personality Disorders in Modern Life* (New York: Wiley, 2000). For a summary of this work, see Richard P. Halgin and Susan Krauss Whitbourne, *Abnormal Psychology: Clinical Perspectives on Psychological Disorders* (4th ed.; Boston: McGraw Hill, 2003), 349.

The unprincipled narcissist thinks none of the rules applies to him even though others must meticulously obey every single rule. Lying, cheating, and stealing are all permitted to him without fault, accountability, or consequence. Others are to blame for whatever unprincipled behavior he exhibits.

The compensatory narcissist plays the part of the superior and exceptional individual but in reality is a toddler who is not really able to accomplish very much. By projecting an image that is exactly opposite of who he really is, he compensates for his lack of true and genuine accomplishments.

Narcissists play many of these roles that are often overlapping and not easy to classify. Narcissists are therefore initially difficult to unmask, identify, and recognize, but the diagnostic criteria developed by the American Psychiatric Association help in the identification.

In its *Diagnostic and Statistical Manual of Mental Disorders*, the American Psychiatric Association defines narcissism as "a pervasive pattern of grandiosity (in fantasy or behaviour), need for admiration, and lack of empathy, beginning by early adulthood and present in various contexts." This disorder is indicated by five (or more) of the following:

- has a grandiose sense of self-importance (e.g., exaggerates achievements and talents, expects to be recognized as superior without commensurate achievements)

- is preoccupied with fantasies of unlimited success, power, brilliance, beauty, or ideal love
- believes that he or she is "special" and unique and can only be understood by, should only be treated by, or should associate with, other special or high-status people (or institutions)
- requires excessive admiration
- has a sense of entitlement, i.e., unreasonable expectations of especially favorable treatment or automatic compliance with his or her expectations
- is interpersonally exploitative, i.e., takes advantage of others to achieve his or her own ends
- lacks empathy: is unwilling to identify with the feelings and needs of others
- is often envious of others or believes that others are envious of him or her
- shows arrogant, haughty behaviors or attitudes."[3]

Many who read this list may identify with one or another of these criteria, but to be diagnosed with a Narcissistic Personality Disorder, an individual must exhibit at least 5 of these characteristics as patterns of behavior and suffer from some form of impairment in job performance or in other areas of life. Both the number and the degree to which someone

[3] American Psychiatric Association, *Diagnostic and Statistical Manual of Mental Disorders* (4th edition; Washington D.C.: American Psychiatric Association, 2000), 301.81.

displays these characteristics determine the severity of his narcissism. Those who show these characteristics primarily in relation to their physical appearance are called "Somatic Narcissists" while those who primarily show them through their intellect are described as "Cerebral Narcissists." These categories, however, are not mutually exclusive.

It is important to recognize that many who haven't been or can't be diagnosed as having a Narcissistic Personality Disorder can nevertheless exhibit narcissistic traits. These individuals have a narcissistic personality and can therefore be called narcissists.[4] The narcissistic personality is far more common than the full-blown disorder. Both, however, are toxic to marriages.

A woman's voice:

"I knew something was wrong with Clint right from the start of our marriage. I worked hard to understand what made him the man he was. I thought if I could understand that, I could figure out how to change him or at least feel better about accepting him for what he was. He was so needy but convinced me that he could take care of himself. Boy, was that a lie. It ended up that I was completely supporting him. Now, I'm a giver and a fixer. I thought I could give him what he needed and fix him, but I couldn't. In the process of concentrating on his needs and fixing him, I lost any sense of who I was, what I needed, and what I wanted out of life. After death finally released me from him, I'm now in therapy as I try to put my life back together after placing it on hold for the past 32 years."

---

[4] Twenge and Campbell, *The Narcissism Epidemic*, 22-23.

While the definition and these criteria are helpful, a woman trapped in a relationship with a narcissist is not really interested in clinically diagnosing her partner. Instead, she simply wants to understand how he came to be the way he is and what makes him tick with the hope that the answers to these two questions will enable her to change him or at least accept and deal with what she can't change. Both her attempt to change him and her acceptance of him, however, cause her to loose her own identity. So, what makes someone a narcissist?

Explanations about the origin of narcissism are various but generally assume that all human beings begin as narcissists and are incapable of attending to the needs of others. A baby knows what it wants and when it wants it but has no conception of or concern about the needs of its mother or others.

As a baby grows to the toddler stage, this me-only mentality continues. A toddler focuses only on what interests him. When a parent says that it's time for a bath or bedtime, the toddler frequently ignores the parent. When forced to comply, the toddler may cry, whine, or throw a tantrum fit. For a toddler, the whole world exists for him and his needs, and he's incapable of considering a larger context. For whatever reasons, the narcissist gets stuck at this stage of development and progresses no further.

One explanation by psychodynamic psychologists is that the toddler's primary care-giver does not empathetically nurture the toddler to shed his self-centered, selfish disposition.[5] The care-giver's emotional distance from the toddler does not permit the toddler to bond appropriately and develop empathy for the care-giver.

Rather than restraining his sense of entitlement, a care-giver enables him to continue thinking the whole world revolves around him. Rather than talking with him about his anger, fear, insecurities, or frustrations, the care-giver avoids emotional encounters with him and simply ignores or excuses his emotions and behavior or does his bidding to avoid his emotional outbursts. The toddler learns by example to ignore the feelings of others. Nothing matters except what he feels and what he wants.

Some psychodynamic psychologists propose a narcissistic turn in the toddler usually as a result of a traumatic event in which a primary care-giver does not show empathy for the toddler.[6] This traumatic event could be something as benign as a bath. A care-giver draws a tub of water and places the toddler into it. The water is a little too warm, and the toddler begins to feel that he's being scalded. He stands up and screams out. The

---

[5] Les Carter, *Enough about You, Let's Talk about Me: How to Recognize and Manage the Narcissists in Your Life* (San Francisco: Jossey-Bass A Wiley Imprint, 2005), 25-30.

[6] Sam Vaknin, *Malignant Self Love: Narcissism Revisited* (Prague & Skopje: Narcissus Publications, 2003), 256-257. See also pages 243-268 for an extended discussion of the making of a narcissist.

care-giver feels the water, but the water temperature while warm does not feel hot to the care-giver who does not remove him from the tub but says to the toddler, "The water is fine. Now, sit down and stop your screaming."

At this moment, the scared toddler turns inward. He does not feel he can trust others around him but must control every situation himself if he's to survive. He directs all his energies to manipulating others so that he remains in control. The care-giver's lack of empathy for him convinces him that no one really cares for him and his needs, and he must assume responsibility for taking what he needs from others without empathy or conscience. By ignoring his frantic screams and protests as he feels he's being scalded, his care-giver negates his existence, and the toddler becomes fixated on affirming his own existence by satisfying his own needs and desires at any cost.

Perhaps, a single event such as this one is too simplistic to explain the narcissistic turn, and several such events are more likely the cause. A care-giver who lacks empathy and is insensitive to the child is likely to act this way repeatedly and subject the toddler to such treatment over and over again.

There is another but quite different explanation, however, about the origin of narcissism. Behavioral psychologists identify the cause as overindulgent, weak parents and a culture that places too much emphasis on self-esteem and self-admiration. According to this view, parents who tell their children that they are special even without any real accomplishments contribute to narcissistic traits in their children. Allowing children to be in control and to get whatever they want also enhances their narcissistic tendencies. Parental and cultural reinforcement of self-esteem and self-admiration confirm a toddler's sense of selfishness and entitlement and feeling that the entire world revolves around him and his needs and desires.[7]

Behavioral psychologists say that narcissists behave as though they're the only ones that matter because they really feel that way. Instead of having low self-esteem, narcissists have an inflated sense of themselves that doesn't match their real abilities or accomplishments. This behavioral explanation is very different from the psychodynamic one, and explanations about the origins of narcissism thus differ significantly.

Perhaps, these explanations about the origin of narcissism help a woman trapped in a relationship with a narcissist to understand what made him the way he is, but her more pressing question is what makes him tick. Seeing him as a two-year-old toddler is perhaps the best way to understand a narcissist.

Toddlers lack empathy, and this trait becomes a deciding factor in narcissism. The degree to which a narcissist lacks empathy determines whether he'll be mildly narcissistic with only certain traits or more severely narcissistic, even to the

---

[7] Twenge and Campbell, *The Narcissism Epidemic*, 73-255.

point of having the full-blown disorder or being a sociopath or serial-killer.

Empathy is what makes us human. It causes us to stop what we are doing or saying when we see that we're hurting someone else. The narcissist lacks empathy and is therefore capable of doing and saying the most cruel and hurtful things imaginable. Even though a wife may want him to understand her feelings and desires and to show her empathy, he's incapable. Only his feelings and desires matter just as in the case of a toddler.

Just as a toddler can't conceive of a world or reality beyond his own, so also a narcissistic husband can't escape his own reality. He must recruit the woman in his life to become part of his world rather than experiencing a mutually shared reality with her. Since his perspective is restricted to his own feelings, motivations, and desires, he can't conceive of her acting in any other way than he acts.

One reliable way to know what a narcissist is about is to listen to his accusations against others. A wife may do something, and her husband may say, "You're trying to undermine our marriage." She can be assured that he's the one undermining their marriage. If he accuses her of being disloyal, she can be sure he's the one being disloyal. If he accuses her of being unfaithful, she can have some confidence that he's had or is contemplating an affair of some type. If he accuses her of being cruel, she may be certain that he's the one being cruel. A narcissist's accusations become a mirror into his own thoughts, actions, and motivations. As a toddler, he can only conceive of her acting and thinking as he himself does. He has no other point of reference but himself.

A woman's voice:

"My sister came to visit me one afternoon, and we were sitting on my living room couch and having a pleasant conversation when my husband entered the room and began yelling at me. 'What have you done with my car keys?' he shouted. 'I haven't done anything with them. I haven't even seen them,' I replied. 'Yes, you have!' he angrily shot back at me. 'No, I haven't,' I insisted. Then, he climbed on top of me with his legs straddling my lap. Towering down, he glared at me and said, 'I'm not going to let you up until you admit the truth that you took my car keys.' I glanced at my sister's shocked face, and I felt so ashamed. He knew how much I cared about what others thought of me and that I'd cave in to him rather than continue this humiliating argument in front of my sister. He also knew how much I valued my honesty. He forced me to choose between my concern for what others thought of me and my honesty. To get him off me, I lied and blankly admitted I'd taken his keys. He got off and, a few minutes later, he found his keys on the kitchen counter right where he'd left them."

Just as a toddler tries to control his world, so also a narcissistic husband attempts to control everything and everyone around him. He establishes his control by appointing himself as the authoritative keeper of absolute truth and reality. He makes pronouncements that mustn't be challenged while he requires her to justify and defend every statement she makes.[8]

[8] Carter (*Enough about You*, 82-94) lists some common narcissistic pronouncements such as "You Must Remain Loyal to Me. . . . It's Never My Fault. . . . Don't Tell Anyone About Our Problems. . . . I'm Not Supposed to

He may say, "I know what is best. Do it my way." When she questions if that way is best, he angrily shouts, "How dare you doubt me. You always doubt me. How can I be the husband I'm supposed to be when you don't support me?" If she should ever propose a course of action on her own, however, he responds, "Who appointed you the authoritative decision-maker? Who do you think you are?"

He tolerates no challenge to his agenda and his unilateral decisions. He refuses to compromise and coordinate with her. Instead, she must adjust to him and his way of thinking and doing things as he pronounces himself the uncontested keeper of absolute truth and reality.

A woman's voice:

"Right from the start, I learned very quickly that he'd already determined the script of the melodrama he was producing. Like an overbearing movie director, he scripted everything I was to say, placed me where he wanted me to be, directed my every move, and even determined the clothes I was to wear. I learned that my opinion was of no value and that I always had to be on his page or suffer his rage. When I tried to find my own voice, sometimes he'd argue and argue with me until finally he just wore me down and I'd give in and return to his script. At other times he'd use the silent treatment because he knew how that drove me insane. In one way or another, he always determined how life was supposed to play out, and I was only allowed to play the part he'd scripted for me."

Suffer. . . . I'm the Center of Everything. . . . The Rules Don't Apply to Me. . . . I Know Best—Do It My Way."

The narcissist preys on someone who does not have a good sense of self or a clear sense of boundaries. Low self-esteem attracts the narcissist. The narcissist appears so confident in establishing reality and so interested in the well-being of the other that the other is willing to entrust her entire sense of self to him and his control.

He makes her lose faith in herself, her feelings, and her decision-making abilities so he can be the sole determiner of what should be felt or done on every occasion and in every situation. He wears her down, and she eventually allows him to define her. The torture chamber is now complete, and she's locked inside as the door slams shut while he sits calmly outside firmly in control.

The narcissistic husband maintains his control by various methods of manipulation. In the recruitment stage, he usually begins by praising and complementing. To get her to prepare him a meal, he may say, "You're such a good cook. I'd really like for you to cook dinner for me tonight." He builds her up, and even when expressing his needs, he makes her feel as if he's complimenting her.

After they're married, he resorts to negative methods of manipulation and constantly complains that he deserves better food than she's preparing. Even though they're on a tight budget, he expects the best, most expensive foods. Attempting to avoid the unpleasantness of his criticisms, she works harder and harder to please him and to meet his unreasonable demands.

As his criticisms become increasingly harsh, his grip on her becomes tighter and tighter.

A woman's voice:

"The invention of the cell phone has made my life even more miserable. Before I had a cell phone, my husband would phone me several time a day at home. If I didn't answer, he'd repeatedly call until I did, and then I had to explain why I didn't answer earlier. If I went out, I had to tell him where I was going and when I'd return home. He'd phone home at exactly the time I said I'd return, and if I didn't answer, I'd catch hell. At least when I was out shopping or running errands, I was somewhat free from him for a brief moment, and I could relax and let down my guard a little. Now that I have a cell phone, however, I'm never free. No matter what I'm doing, I must answer or he flips out and yells and rages when he returns home from work, my worst time of the day."

To maintain his control, he manipulates her expectation that marriage should be a give and take and that compromise and approval are essential. He enslaves her into trying to secure his cooperation and approval. He may say, "If you were more caring, more giving, and more concerned about pleasing me, I could be more cooperative. That is the kind of husband I want to be, but you're not letting me." Since he decides when he'll cooperate and to what he'll give his approval, he maintains constant control.

Non-narcissistic people are fairly consistent in giving their cooperation and approval, but not the narcissist. When it suits him, he cooperates. When it doesn't, he becomes obstinate. When it suits him, he gives his approval. When it doesn't, he doesn't. A wife can never predict when he will and when he won't. His inconsistency is his way of keeping her off balance and himself in control. He uses her desire for cooperation and approval to enslave her to his absolute control.

A woman's voice:

"Gifts? He showered me with gifts but never what I wanted. If I said I wanted a pant-suit, he'd buy me a dress and then explain to me that he thought I looked better in dresses than pant suits. If I said I wanted a granite countertop for my kitchen, he'd buy me a quartz countertop and try to convince me that quartz was much more practical than granite. My closet, my bedroom, my entire house is full of gifts that he wanted me to have. Gift-giving was his way of getting what he wanted, not what I wanted. My desires didn't count. Gift-giving was his way of controlling me. If I ever even hinted of doing something independently of him, he'd berate me and ask, 'How could you even think of doing that after all I've given to you?' He made me feel as though I were so ungrateful for all his gifts, but how could I be grateful for gifts that I never wanted in the first place?"

The Greek philosopher Aristotle observed that humans are motivated by pain and pleasure and are drawn to pleasure but try to avoid pain. The narcissistic husband knows this truth only too well. By dishing out pleasure and pain, he can control and manipulate his wife to do his bidding and even to think his thoughts.

As she complies with his wishes, he may bestow empty praise on her or at least withhold pain momentarily. If she should ever cross him or have a thought of her own, however, he knows how to make her life a living hell as he shames and humiliates her until she gives in to his demands.

Even her compliance, however, does not lead to the peace she so desperately seeks, for he becomes increasingly more demanding no matter what she does. He knows how to wear her down by his relentless arguments and unpredictable outbursts of anger and rage.

A woman's voice:

"When I met Kevin, I thought I'd found my soul mate. He appeared so assertive, confident, and self-assured. He seemed to be everything I was not, and I thought he'd complete me. Even though our courtship had some conflicts, I attributed them to the normal stresses of a relationship. Our honeymoon was a fairytale-dream-come-true. When we returned, he said to me, 'The honeymoon's over. Now, I want to be surrounded with beauty so you'll wear no clothes in my house.' I was so shocked that I thought he was kidding, but he wasn't. When I tried to explain that I felt uncomfortable being naked all the time, he responded that my feelings were misguided. He stated that I was his wife and I had a responsibility to satisfy his eyes with beauty. If I didn't comply, he threatened to find someone else who would. That scared me because I didn't want to fail in my marriage. So I took off my clothes and for several years went naked around the house. The only time I was permitted to wear clothes was when we had company. When I tried to wear clothes at other times, he'd yell, rage, and belittle me as the most ungrateful and insensitive wife ever for not meeting his needs. His eyes deserved beauty, and I had to supply it or else. I felt so vulnerable without clothes, and the humiliation of nakedness took a heavy toll on my emotions and sense of self until I couldn't take it anymore and left."

When all else fails, he may threaten to take her children from her or keep her from seeing them. He continues his manipulations until she's totally and completely under his control and emptied of her entire self and becomes nothing but an extension of him and his miserable existence.

In addition to control, one of the most defining characteristics of a narcissist and what makes him tick is his intense need to validate his false existence and his inflated sense of self by "self-regulation strategies" or by procuring "narcissistic supply."[9]

Self-regulation strategies refer to all those attempts by a narcissist to regulate or maintain his self-admiration by manipulating others. A narcissist feels that he is superior to others, and that he is special, entitled, and unique when he really isn't. Others then become instruments that he uses to maintain his illusory self. By convincing others that he is special, he validates his own self-admiration. His self-regulation strategies feed his self-admiration, and his appetite for this validation is constant and insatiable.

Similar to self-regulation strategies, narcissistic supply is the emotional response and confirmation the narcissist manipulates and elicits from others. Although everyone needs affirming emotional responses from other people, the narcissist's need is over-the-top and is never really satisfied. Vaknin calls the narcissist "the mental equivalent of an alcoholic."[10]

---

[9] For self-regulation strategies, see Twenge and Campbell, *The Narcissism Epidemic*, 19, 213. For an extended discussion of narcissistic supply, see Vaknin, *Malignant Self Love*, 454-460.

[10] Vaknin, *Malignant Self Love*, 454.

The narcissist is addicted to the attention and affirmation of others. He desperately needs their confirmation of the projected image of his false self, and he can't live without it just as an alcoholic thinks he can't live without his alcohol. The narcissist devotes all his energies and time to securing this narcissistic supply.

He manipulates others into congratulating, applauding, praising, and honoring the false self that he's projected. This supply deludes the narcissist into thinking that his false self is his true self, but the supply must be continuous, for if it ever stops, his true self threatens his false self. The very existence of his false self, his very existence, is brought into question.

If the narcissist can't secure positive affirmation, he resorts to eliciting negative responses as narcissistic supply. While narcissists may prefer positive emotional responses from others, negative responses work just as well to validate his false self. If the narcissistic husband can manipulate his wife into feeling and expressing fear, frustration, anger, or even hatred, he feels affirmed. By controlling her emotions and her emotional responses, even negative ones, the projected sense of his false self as the "adult" in control is secured.

A wife may wonder why her husband is always so contentious with her and ready to pick a fight about everything. The reason he's as he is, the reason he acts as he does, what makes him tick is his need for narcissistic supply. Like an alcoholic or drug addict, he'll do or say anything to get it no matter how miserable it makes her and others around him feel.

The narcissist is so dependent on narcissistic supply for sustaining his false image that he must recruit and maintain a large number of people as sources. He's almost irresistible as he courts them for narcissistic supply. The problem is that his need is so all-consuming that they're eventually used up or emptied out and have little or no emotion left to give.

At this point, they stop supplying the emotional responses the narcissist needs and he discards them as easily as an old worn out pair of shoes. After all, he didn't really have a mutual relationship with them in the first place. In fact, a narcissist is incapable of entering and sustaining mutual relationships. Others were simply recruited to give him narcissistic supply. If they pull back their emotional responses, they're of no use to him any longer, and the narcissist leaves them behind without a thought and moves on to recruit other sources.

Since friends and colleagues can easily walk away, the narcissist prefers family members and especially a wife and children as sources of his narcissistic supply. It's difficult for a wife and almost completely impossible for young children to escape his manipulative efforts to secure narcissistic supply from them.

When a wife is completely used up, she may resort to alcoholism, drug abuse, suicide, or divorce. Of all these options, divorce is of course the best, but children can't really exercise this option.[11] If she has children with him, even divorce may not end his attempts to use her and her children as a source for his narcissistic supply.

A woman's voice:

"During the first stages of our separation, I overheard Mike talking to our two-year-old daughter about how I wanted to leave them. I plugged in the baby monitor so I could hear more clearly what he was saying to her because it seemed he was telling her things that were untrue. Mike must have realized that I was trying to listen because he came running into the room, ripped the monitor from the outlet, completely separating the wire from the plug and whipped me with the dangling broken cord and left searing red marks on my legs. How can I raise this child with him?"

As important as self-regulation strategies and narcissistic supply are for explaining what makes a narcissist tick, a wife who wants to understand her narcissistic husband simply can't overlook his refusal to take responsibility for his actions. He sees himself as the sane, rational person forced to deal with problems created by others who are incompetent and defective.

---

[11] Books dealing with the children of narcissists are usually written for the children after they become adults. See Nina W. Brown, *Children of the Self-Absorbed: A Grownup's Guide to Getting over Narcissistic Parents* (Oakland, CA: New Harbinger's Publications, Inc.) and Susan Forward with Craig Buck, *Toxic Parents: Overcoming Their Hurtful Legacy and Reclaiming Your Life* (New York: Bantam, 2002). A related book on this topic is Stephanie Donaldson-Pressman and Robert M. Pressman, *The Narcissistic Family: Diagnosis and Treatment* (San Francisco: Jossey-Bass, 1994). Vaknin's discussion (*Malignant Self Love*, 488-492) is also relevant. A book written for younger children of a narcissistic parent would be helpful.

Whatever the problem, it's not his fault and someone else is surely to blame as he portrays himself as the innocent victim of the situation. When confronted, he reverses the charge and makes her guilty of whatever she's accusing him. When confronted, he shifts the blame to her. For a wife, this feature of narcissism is particularly maddening. In her every encounter with him, shared responsibility is impossible, and it's always her fault.

Two metaphors help to explain what makes a narcissistic husband tick. First, the narcissist is an emotional tornado-maker. He throws everyone off balance and off their foundations just as a tornado does. As everyone swirls around him, he calmly sits in the eye of the tornado and spins the emotions of everyone else to the point of their emotional exhaustion. He blows everyone else off balance emotionally so he can control every situation and everyone in that situation.

A woman's voice:

"Lying in the snow while wearing shorts and t-shirt, I stare up at the stars and scream repeatedly as I cry inside my head, 'HELP ME LORD! I CAN'T DEAL WITH HIM ANYMORE! HELP ME LORD! I'M GOING TO DIE! HELP ME LORD, I'M GOING INSANE!' Then, the calm after the storm. . . . I think I'll just lie here a little longer in the snow. It's better than going back inside his house."

He knows how to press all the right buttons to keep everyone swirling in the devastating storm he's created. If his wife should try to gain her footing, he quickly accuses her of being unreasonable, insensitive, foolish, or stupid. By throwing her and everyone else off balance, he sits firmly in control as his tornado blows everyone else first this way and then that. The narcissist is an expert tornado-maker.

Second, the narcissistic husband is a black hole. He draws everything into himself. Resources, emotions, everything is sucked in, but nothing comes out. While consuming vast amounts of resources, the narcissist returns little or nothing to anyone else. All resources are consumed to sustain his illusory self-image and are not available for accomplishing tasks or goals or anything else.

Pity the poor woman who is drawn into his gravitational pull from which even light does not escape. Whereas she can spend no money on clothes, he's dressed in the finest. Whereas he buys an expensive bicycle for himself, she gets a used one from a garage sale. Whereas second-hand and second-rate are good enough for her, he's entitled to the best of everything. He is and functions as a black hole.

So, what makes a narcissistic husband tick? A wife can be certain that in every encounter with him, he's a two-year-old toddler intent on establishing his control, in procuring narcissistic supply, and in deflecting blame from himself. When his lack of empathy is thrown into this mix, the recipe for a toxic narcissistic relationship is complete.

The narcissistic husband will callously erode his wife's feelings, thoughts, and plans as he establishes himself as the sole keeper of absolute truth and reality. He'll coldly empty her of all her emotional feelings as he elicits his narcissistic supply. He'll cruelly blame her for everything and leave her wondering about her own sanity and balance. If she looks behind his mask, this infantile, self-centered, all-about-me approach to every situation is how a narcissistic husband ticks, and of this she can be certain.

A wife assumes that by knowing what made her husband the way he is and what makes him tick, she can change him. In this assumption, she couldn't be more wrong. Nothing she can do will ever change him. Appeasing him does not work but only makes him more arrogant that he can control her.

If she thinks that getting him into counseling will produce change in him, she needs to think carefully about some realistic facts. Narcissists resist going to counseling because of course nothing is ever their fault. The problems lie with everyone else who needs counseling, not them.

If a wife succeeds in getting her narcissistic husband into counseling, he's probably not there to gain the self-awareness that will lead him to change and modify his behavior to make their home-life better. No, he's there to manipulate the situation and enlist the counselor as an ally in his attempt to control her. He's there to elicit more narcissistic supply from her and to confirm that all their problems are her fault. If her narcissistic husband realizes that he can't manipulate the counselor, he's finished with counseling and probably won't return.

A woman's voice:

"'Hi,' I said as I walked up to a teller at the bank where my husband Rob worked. The teller looked nervous and gave me a strange look as I approached her. She responded, 'Oh, hey, are you here to see Rob?' 'Well, not really,' I answered, 'I just need to deposit this check into our account.' The teller worked quickly on my transaction and then started speaking in a quiet tone, 'Did Rob tell you that his secretary quit last week?' I shook my head, and she continued, 'I'm sure it was because of the tension in the office due to the sexual harassment complaint she filed against Rob about a month ago.' My heart skipped a beat, and I know that my eyes revealed my surprise to hear this news. Rob hadn't told me about any of this incident, so I was shocked and embarrassed, but I tried to pretend like I knew what she was talking about just to get the conversation over with. I left the bank without talking to Rob because I knew that this kind of discussion needed to take place at home. When Rob returned home that evening, I was so scared to bring up the subject because it seemed that our discussions always turned into intense arguments and it also seemed that I turned out to be the horrible person in the end. However, it was important for me to know about what happened at the bank, so I asked him, 'Have you had some problem with your secretary at work? The teller mentioned to me today that she quit because of a sexual harassment suit. Is that right?' He snapped back, 'What are you doing going behind my back and talking to a teller at my bank? How could you snoop on me like that? How could you not trust me after all I've done for you?' Feeling more overwhelmed, I answered, 'I wasn't snooping. The teller just brought it up while I was there today, and I felt silly that I hadn't heard anything about it.' He shot back, 'Well, I'm appalled that you were checking up on me and talking about me behind my back. I'm going to quit the bank anyway because they're so horrible about my schedule and they don't pay me what I'm worth. Anyway, let's get back to your trust issues. You know I'd never do anything like that so why are you accusing me? You always think the worst about everything! He shrieked, 'I think you owe me an apology!' This conversation went on and on like this, and I ended up feeling guilty and horrible and apologized and felt even worse about everything and especially about myself."

Devoid of empathy, the narcissistic husband lacks the one quality that could enable him to modify his behavior and change. Unlike Jim Carey as Stanley Ipkiss, he can't simply remove his mask and throw it away but is trapped in the reflection of the illusory image that he's created and must constantly project and protect.

Neither is his wife able to remove the mask for him even if she understands why he's as he is and what makes him tick. He probably won't change, and she'll spare herself much anguish and frustration if she abandons her expectations that he will.

Her choices are very limited. She may remain hopelessly incarcerated in the torture chamber he's created for her or she may try to escape and end or at least restrict her toxic association with him. If she decides she wants out of his relational toxicity, he often recruits and manipulates three powerful guards to stand at the door of her torture chamber and prevent her escape.

One of these three guards is the biblical teaching of male headship and female submission. The second is the church's interpretation of the words of Jesus that prohibit divorce, and the third is the biblical teaching that encourages wives to expect the miracle of his transformation by her patient suffering.

Faced with such formidable guards and her husband's ability to recruit many others to his cause against her, she's far too often beaten down, demoralized, and forced to remain in a toxic narcissistic relationship with him. In contradiction to their essential nature, the Bible and the church are co-opted by the narcissist to serve as preservatives of his toxic narcissistic recipe.

Part 1 has described this recipe, and now Part 2 considers a woman's choice to leave and examines the Bible and the church as preservatives to determine if the narcissist's use of them to keep her under his control is genuine and authentic or, like everything else in his life, a lie and a deception.

Part 2

The Preservatives in the Toxic Narcissistic Recipe

Chapter 3
Male Headship and Female Submission

The Bible is the one book that has most influenced western civilization, and it affects almost everyone, even those who do not profess a faith tradition based on the Bible. Nowhere is the Bible's influence more evident than in the traditional assumption that the husband is the head, leader, and boss of his wife and that she's supposed to be submissive to him. Both of these notions preserve toxic narcissistic relationships since they play into the narcissistic husband's sense of entitlement and superiority and his pathological need for control.

A Sister's Story

My sister and I had always been close; that is, until she married Mark. He belonged to an ultra-conservative church and insisted that she attend with him since his entire family belonged to that church. Growing up, we had our own church, but our church was not good enough for him. He was constantly criticizing our church and pointing out how our church had missed the true message of the Bible.

He had certain biblical passages to which he frequently referred. He recited them so often that I can almost quote them from memory. He loved to quote 1 Corinthians 11:3, where the Apostle Paul writes, "Now I want you to understand that the head of every man is Christ, the head of a woman is her husband, and the head of Christ is God." Another verse he loved to quote was Ephesians 5:23, which reads, "For the husband is the head of the wife just as Christ is the head of his church" (Ephesians 5:23).

He'd couple these verses with others that speak of female submission such as Colossians 3:18, which commands, "Wives submit to your own husbands as is fitting in the Lord," and 1 Peter 2:17, which commands its readers to honor all and then specifies that wives honor all "by submitting to their own husbands" (3:1). He also cited another verse. I believe it was from Ephesians, but I can't remember it exactly.[1]

At any rate, Mark asserted that our church ignored these verses but that his church held true to them. He insisted that my sister assume her God-ordained subservient role and submit to his headship. The Bible, he claimed, gave him the right to be her leader and gave her the responsibility to obey him in everything. Because she was such a people-pleaser, she gave in to his demands.

---

[1] Ephesians 5:22.

As I saw my sister sink further and further under his control, I became increasingly concerned. Her otherwise care-free and happy demeanor gave way to a pensive nervousness that I'd never before seen in her. She'd always had some trouble making decisions, but now she'd not even make the most minor decision without clearing it with Mark first.

When I tried to talk to her about what was happening, she muttered, "Mark thinks that he's supposed to be in charge of me."

"But what do you think?" I asked.

"He must be right," she answered, "for the Bible and the pastor at his church say so. I'm just trying to fulfill the role God has assigned me."

I thought and thought about her answer. I wondered how the Bible, a minister, and even God could assign someone to such a demeaning role. I'd been taught that God created humans with free will and that decision-making was essential to being human. In her marriage, my sister was more like a puppet or robot than a human being.

Something seemed really wrong to me, and I decided to talk to my pastor about it to see what he'd say. After explaining my problem and my sister's situation to him, he advised me to see a certain professor at the local university. I called the number he gave me and made an appointment.

I was somewhat nervous about speaking with this professor and wondered if he'd talk over my head and try to impress me with big words. When I arrived at his office, he quickly put me at ease. He was so friendly and kind and listened attentively as I explained my problem with the whole biblical headship thing, at least the way Mark understood it, and with my sister's subservience.

I asked this professor point blank if Mark's interpretation of those biblical passages were correct. He smiled as he responded, "Many indeed interpret these passages as you've described Mark's understanding, and it's not at all unusual for a church such as Mark's to use these verses to establish a relationship such as Mark and your sister have."

"But are they right?" I asked.

"Well, they fail to take some important facts into consideration," he answered.

"What facts?" I asked.

"Take Paul's statement that the husband is the head of his wife," he continued. "Mark and those like him naively assume that the head is the center of decision-making and controls the body."

"But it certainly is," I interrupted.

He nodded his head and said, "For us, yes, but not for the people in Paul's time." He then reached up and pulled a large book from his shelf, opened it, and began to read a passage from the Greek philosopher Aristotle. This passage identified not the head, but the heart as the organ that controlled the body.[2]

"That point of view really seems absurd," I said.

Again, he nodded his head and said, "To us, yes, but not to those people. The vast majority of them agreed with Aristotle, and the common view was that the heart, not the head, controls the body."

"Did anyone understand the correct view that the head really is the control center?" I asked.

He replied, "Yes, a few beginning with the physician Alcmaeon and continuing through Plato.[3] The issue of whether the heart or the head controlled the body was hotly debated by many well known figures from the ancient world.[4] It was not until about a century after the Apostle Paul, however, that the

---

[2] Aristotle, *On the Parts of Animals* 656a16-30. See also *On the Generation of Animals* 740a19-20. For other texts that present the heart as the control center of the body, see Hippocrates, *On the Heart* 10,12, which reads, "For the organ by which a human perceives and knows is formed in the left cavity of the heart and rules the rest of the soul," and Hippocrates, *On the Nature of Bones* 19,6-9, which explains, "Both the former blood vessels and these vessels fall into the heart, for the heart is settled in the narrow space of the passage as though it holds the reins from all the body. Therefore also, the sense perception of all the body is most of all around the chest."

[3] Plato, *Timaeus* 44d.

[4] For summaries of this debate and the names of the participants, see Anonymi Medici *On Acute and Chronic Illnesses* 1,1-19 and Aêtius (Pseudo-Plutarch) *On the Doctrines of the Philosophers* 899a1-899b4.

head came to be generally recognized as the control center of the body."

"At that time, the famous physician Galen engaged in debates with philosophers in Rome.[5] He'd bring live animals to these debates and would cut into them and manipulate portions of their brain to get them to move various parts of their body. His persuasive object lessons won the day and refuted these philosophers who held that the heart controlled the body. From that time to this, the head has been considered as the control center of the body."

"All of that is kind of interesting," I said, "but how does it relate to my problem?"

"Well, he replied, "your problem is with Paul's statement that the husband is the head of his wife, right?"

"Yes," I answered.

"Then we need to know what Paul thought about the head. If Mark and his church are correct in their assessment that Paul meant the husband controls his wife, then Paul must have stood on the minority side of this ancient debate with those who held the head to control the body. If, however, Paul stood on the majority side with those who thought the heart and not the head controlled the body, then Mark and his church can't be correct in their interpretation of what Paul meant."

---

[5] Galen, *On the Doctrines of Hippocrates and Plato* 7,3,10,7-7,3,12,1.

I was beginning to see where this professor was going with all this, and so I eagerly asked, "What did Paul think?"

He again reached up to his bookshelf and pulled down a Bible and said, "Read for yourself." He helped me find several passages in Paul's letters. I can't recall them all now, but in every one of them Paul used the word heart when he spoke of thinking and decision-making.[6] Oh, sometimes the English translation I was reading would use the word *mind*, but this professor assured me that the word Paul actually used was the Greek word for *heart*.

"You see," he said, "if Paul really meant to say that the husband controls his wife, Paul should have said that the husband is the heart of his wife, for Paul believed that the heart is the center of intelligence and controls the body. Of course, Paul doesn't say that because he doesn't mean it. Instead, he says that the husband is the head of his wife."

---

[6] See Romans 1:21, where the Apostle Paul writes, "Although they knew God, they didn't honor or give thanks to Him as God, but they became foolish in their reasoning and their stupid hearts were darkened." See 1 Corinthians 2:9, where Paul approvingly quotes the scripture, "No eye has seen, nor ear heard, nor the human heart conceived what God has prepared for those who love him." See 1 Corinthians 4:5, where Paul warns, "So, don't judge anything before its time until the Lord comes who also will enlighten the secrets of darkness and reveal the counsels of hearts." See 2 Corinthians 3:15, where Paul explains, "But to this day, whenever Moses is read, a veil lies upon their heart." See also 2 Corinthians 9:7, where Paul instructs, "Let each give just as each has purposed in his heart."

"Wow," I said, "So Mark's contention that Paul calls the husband the head of his wife and means that the husband controls his wife is just wrong."

"Seriously problematic," he answered. "Mark, his church, and everyone else who holds this view fail to consider that Paul didn't think the head is the control center of the body."

"Okay," I said. "Then what does Paul mean when he says that the husband is the head of his wife?"

"Well, definitely not control," he answered. "Consider how the people of Paul's time must have perceived the function of the head if it didn't control the body. What does the body need to live?"

I thought for a moment and then responded, "The basics. Food, water, and air, of course."

He asked, "And what part of the body supplies these necessities to the body; I mean, where do these necessities enter the body?"

I again thought for a moment and then answered, "Air enters through the nose and mouth, and food and water only through the mouth."

"Correct," he said, "and the nose and mouth are both parts of the head, aren't they?"

"Indeed they are," I answered.

He continued, "What quality of life would the body have without seeing, hearing, smelling, and tasting?"

"Not a very desirable one," I responded.

Again, he continued, "The eyes, the ears, the nose, and the tongue are all parts of the head. Those people thus understood the function of the head as supplying what the body needs to live and to live well. When Paul says that the husband is the head of his wife, Paul means that the husband is the *source* for all his wife needs to live and to thrive."

"Wow, that's certainly a different understanding than Mark and his church have," I blurted out. "They understand that the wife is there more for her husband rather than his being there for her, and my sister certainly hasn't been thriving under Mark's domination and oppressive control."

Knowing that if I brought any of this up to Mark, he'd challenge me, I asked the professor, "How can we be so sure Paul meant that the husband as head is the *source* of all that his wife needs to live and to live well?"

Again, the professor reached for the Bible, opened it to a passage Mark was so fond of quoting, and the professor began reading. He didn't stop reading, however, where Mark usually stopped but continued reading past 1 Corinthians 11:3 to verse 12, which says, "For just as woman came from man so also man is born through the agency of a woman, but all things are from God."

The professor pointed out that right after Paul states that the husband is the head of his wife, Paul resorts to source language and talks about the mutual source of women and men. He explained, "According to Genesis 2:18-24, the first woman was taken from the first man so Paul can say that woman came from man. According to Genesis 4:1-2, however, men are born from women so Paul can say that man is born through the agency of a woman. The basis of the two genders' mutual source, however, is God since all things are from God."

Then, the professor turned to another of Mark's favorite passages, but again the professor kept reading past Ephesians 5:23 to verses 25-29, which command:

> Husbands, love your wives just as Christ also loved the church and gave himself for it so that he might sanctify it after he purified it by the washing of water by the word so that he himself might present the church to himself honored and not having spot or wrinkle or any other such things but so that she might be holy and blameless. Thus, husbands should love their own wives as they love their own bodies. He who loves his own wife loves himself, for no one has ever hated his own flesh but nourishes it and cares for it and cherishes it just as Christ nourishes and cherishes the church.

Again, the professor pointed out that in this passage, Paul resorts to source language after stating that the husband is the head of his wife. The professor emphasized, "What Paul means when he says that the husband is the head of his wife is that the husband must put aside his own needs so he can provide his wife with what she needs just as Christ didn't place his own life first but gave himself on behalf of his church. If Mark truly wants to be the head, he must be the *source* of what your sister needs to live and to thrive."

Shaking my head in disbelief, I said, "That's just the opposite of what Mark and his church think."

The professor also shook his head and said, "Yes, they have unfortunately overlooked some important facts."

I sat silently for a moment as I relished the thought of setting Mark straight about his true role as my sister's head. My pleasant little daydream was interrupted, however, as I suddenly remembered that Mark not only quoted these biblical passages about his headship but also other passages about how my sister was supposed to submit to him. I knew I'd taken a lot of the professor's time, but I wanted to know if Mark was also somehow misusing these verses about wives' submitting to their husbands. So, I asked the professor about submission.

Again, he shook his head and said, "Mark, his church, and others like them read the *submission* mentioned in these passages as *subservience*."

"What's the difference?" I asked.

"Very much indeed," he said, "*Subservience* means to serve or act in a subordinate capacity. It implies slavery and oppression and refers to a condition of servitude in which a person is reduced to a slave. In contrast, *submission* refers to a voluntary placing of oneself with another person or fitting into a larger whole. These texts speak of a wife's submission to her husband but not her servitude since in each of these passages, slaves are addressed in a separate section.[7] Instead of recommending that a wife slavishly obey her husband without question in a subservient way as Mark and his church do, these texts recommend that she submit to her husband, and submission is very different from subservience. All of this is confirmed by the Greek term *hupotasso*, which is translated by *submit* or *submission* but really means *to fit in*, but I'll spare you the linguistic details," he said.

I was somewhat grateful since I do not know Greek and figured that any such discussion was a little beyond me. However, I did want to know more about the notion of submission so I asked him if he could give me an example of submission so I could understand it better.

"Of course," he said.

I think he was really enjoying our conversation as much as I was. He acted as though he had all this knowledge stored up but never had anyone who wanted to listen to him talk about it. Believe me, I was listening because I had already seen how his knowledge could really help my sister out of the jam she was in.

I listened attentively as he continued speaking, "A good example is actually given in one of the passages that speak about submission." He reached once again for the Bible and opened it to 1 Peter 3:1-6, another passage I recognized that

---

[7] Colossians 3:22-25; 1 Peter 2:18-25; Ephesians 6:5-8.

Mark liked to quote. [8] The professor showed me that Sarah, Abraham's wife, is presented in this passage as the model of submission, and then he began to talk about Sarah.

"Her relationship with her husband Abraham," he said, "is definitely not one of subservience since Abraham, on various occasions, listens to her and follows her agenda. On one occasion, God even says to Abraham, 'Whatever Sarah says to you, do as she tells you.' [9] Sarah is assertive and anything but a mindless puppet controlled by Abraham's dictates. Her submission to him is demonstrated by her fitting-in with his life's calling and purpose, not by her groveling acquiescence to his demands. She moves with him from Ur of the Chaldees to Haran and then to Canaan, the land God promised to him. She could've complained about the hardships of moving so much, but she doesn't. She adapts herself to his occupation of herding sheep and cattle even though it means she has to live in a tent instead of a house. She could've nagged him about building her a nice house because he had the resources, but she doesn't demand a house. She even bears a child with him in her 90s so he can fulfill God's plan of fathering the chosen people."

---

[8] For the background of this text see Troy W. Martin, "The TestAbr and the Background of 1 Pet 3,6," *Zeitschrift für die neutestamentliche Wissenschaft und die Kunde der älteren Kirche* 90(1999): 139-146.

[9] Genesis 21:12. See also Genesis 16:2; 21:8-14.

The professor continued, "Her life demonstrates that her submission to Abraham consists not in her capitulating to his every whim but in her doing good works and not fearing to help him become successful in his life's calling and purpose. 1 Peter 3:6 states that women become Sarah's daughters if they follow her model of submission by doing good works and fearing no terror."

I thought for a moment about the example of Sarah that the professor had just described, and then I said, "So when Mark insists that my sister submit in cowering fear and without questioning to his every demand, his insistence is very different from the Bible's recommendation for submission."

"Absolutely," the professor responded, "the Bible actually prohibits fear as a motivation for her submission since following Sarah's model of submission requires 'fearing no terror.' Submission means that your sister willingly offers to fit in with her husband's calling and purpose. A wise wife knows that her husband won't be happy unless he finds an occupation and purpose in life that fulfills him, and she's willing to do what it takes to support him in finding his purpose and fulfillment. Your sister's willingness to fit in and help Mark, however, doesn't preclude her own realization of who she is and what she's about in life. By fitting in or submitting to Abraham, Sarah realizes her own role as the ancestor of the people of God and the role model for Godly wives, and your sister's submission to Mark should also enable her to realize her full potential as well."

As I heard the professor say, "Her full potential," I realized that is what I really wanted for my sister. The way Mark had so diminished her by his insistence on his misguided headship and her subservience was what was so troubling to me.

I thanked the professor for his time, and as I left his office, I didn't quite know how I'd ever explain all this to my sister, but I knew the next time Mark brought up these biblical passages that mention male headship and female submission, I wasn't going to sit quietly by and accept his misguided interpretation.

The Narcissist's Headship and Female Submission

A narcissistic husband uses Paul's statements about male headship to support his superiority and dominance over his wife. He uses these statements to project himself as her controller, decision-maker, and leader. According to an informed reading of Paul's statements, however, a husband is the head of his wife if he yields his own needs and desires and supplies what she needs to live and to thrive. He performs his head role not by controlling and dominating her but by meeting her needs.

According to an informed understanding, the biblical teaching of male headship should no longer be used to preserve toxic narcissistic relationships but rather should be used to completely eliminate them. A narcissistic husband may appeal to male headship to preserve his false sense of superiority and elitism and his self-appointed position as ruler and boss of his wife. Such an appeal, however, lacks the support of Paul's true notion of the husband as the source of what his wife needs to thrive. In reality, a narcissistic husband can never be the head of his wife in the Pauline sense because the narcissist can't ever forego his own needs long enough to supply hers.

A woman's voice:

"'I'm the husband,' he would announce proudly as if this meant that he was the boss and I the menial slave. I was there for him, but he was never there for me. I was beneath him, and he made that perfectly clear. I was supposed to support him, but he felt no obligation toward me. Our relationship always operated on a double standard, and I was always on the bottom end of it."

Many narcissistic husbands also use the biblical command for wives to submit to their husbands as a club to keep their wives in submission and under their control. According to an informed reading of the biblical texts, however, submission for a woman married to a narcissistic husband means that she'll not preserve the toxic narcissistic relationship he's established. She'll not participate in his futile attempts to achieve absolute control or engage in his exhausting manipulations for narcissistic supply. To do so is to pervert the very model of submission recommended in the Bible and illustrated by Sarah.

Going with him down the pointless road of his all-about-me existence won't help him achieve his life's calling and purpose. Since he's not likely to aspire to very much beyond his false self, submission for her means asserting her own demands and needs to give him a chance to fulfill his biblical role as head to supply her with what she needs. Even if he chooses to reject the biblical mandate to be her supplier and chooses not to achieve his life's potential or to rise above his narcissism, submission requires her to realize her own calling and purpose in life as best she can.

The biblical teachings of male headship and female submission are often used especially by narcissistic husbands to guard her torture chamber and to preserve the toxic narcissistic relationship he's created. Such use of these biblical teachings is not genuine and authentic but, like everything else in a narcissist's life, a deception. Many indeed have been deceived by readings of biblical texts that do not reflect the liberating intention of the Bible.

Instead of guarding her torture chamber and throwing her back when she tries to escape, the biblical teachings about male headship and female submission actually throw open the door of her torture chamber and call her to freedom from the tyranny of his narcissistic personality and the toxic relationship he's created for her. Seeing this one guard as really assisting rather than hindering her escape, however, doesn't resolve her problem with another even more powerful guard, namely the church's prohibition against divorce.

Chapter 4
The Church's Prohibition against Divorce

For many women trapped in the torture chamber of a toxic narcissistic relationship, their church with its prohibition against divorce is the most formidable guard keeping them locked up and preventing them from escaping. These women frequently hear biblical texts quoted as a justification for the church's stand against divorce. One of the often quoted passages is Malachi 2:16, which reads, "'For I hate divorce,' says the Lord the God of Israel."

Of course, the most often quoted passages are Jesus' pronouncements about divorce. When asked about divorce, Jesus responds, "What God has yoked together, let no one separate" (Matthew 19:6). Jesus continues, "Whoever divorces his wife except for sexual indiscretion and marries another woman commits adultery" (Matthew 19:9). In Mark 10:12, Jesus further states, "If after divorcing her husband, she marries another, she commits adultery."

With none other than the Lord the God of Israel and Jesus being cited as justification for the church's stand against divorce, a woman caught in the hell of a toxic narcissistic relationship is often convinced that the church will offer her little help if she decides to leave her husband.

A woman's voice:

"My ex-husband's constant barrage of demeaning criticism had left me so drained that I'd nothing left to give, and he wanted out of the marriage. He knew that adultery was the only grounds for divorce that our church would recognize so he began to pressure me to have an affair so that he could divorce me and still remain in good standing in the church. I can't believe it now, but I did it. I'm so ashamed now, but at the time I thought it was the only way I could escape from my nightmare."

Sadly, her conviction is more often than not confirmed by her experience. The church and primarily church leaders such as priests and pastors are often so intent on preserving the sanctity of marriage that these leaders frequently overlook their role in preserving toxic narcissistic marriages.

These marriages are inherently abusive because the narcissist is by definition an abuser. As a toddler, he never formed a clear conception of his boundary in relation to the rest of his world. In his mind, the world is but an extension of himself with no boundary in between. Thus, he does not respect the boundaries of others and constantly abuses them by ignoring and violating their boundaries.

The church has been slow to respond to the pervasive abuse that occurs even in Christian marriages. Nancy Nason-Clark asks a probing question, "The Evangelical family is sacred, but is it safe?"[1] Her question pertains not only to Evangelical families but to all religious families.

Because of society's increased awareness of physical and sexual abuse and the recent concept of the *battered woman*, church leaders have become better informed and generally offer more helpful advice to women affected by these types of abuse although a few pastors still unwisely advise women to remain in these dangerous situations.[2] For these few pastors, keeping the marriage intact at least in appearance is the most important priority. Their philosophy seems to be "marriage—for better, for worse, for keeps" no matter what.

Church leaders are less adept at recognizing and addressing other non-physical types of abuse such as verbal and emotional abuse. These types of abuse are often considered less threatening to the marriage when in reality they're far more devastating to a woman than even physical abuse.

The outward wounds of physical abuse eventually heal and garner some sympathy from others. The inward wounds of verbal and emotional abuse are a woman's private hell and remain open sores from which her energies and life-essence

---

[1] Nancy Nason-Clark, "The Evangelical Family Is Sacred, but Is It Safe?" Chapter 8 in *Healing the Hurting: Giving Hope and Help to Abused Women* (Catherine Clark Kroeger and James R. Beck, eds; Grand Rapids: Baker, 1998), 109-125.

[2] Mary Susan Miller, *No Visible Wounds: Identifying Nonphysical Abuse of Women by their Men* (New York: Fawcett Books, 1995), 7.

continually ooze and drain away. Bones mend, bruises disappear, blood stops flowing, but the inward destruction of a woman's true self is much more difficult to mend. The responsible church leader will learn to recognize the nonphysical types of abuse that typically occur in toxic narcissistic relationships and advise women wisely.

The New York State Coalition Against Domestic Violence has a list of questions to assist women and counselors in recognizing abusive behaviors. The list obviously includes questions about physical abuse such as hitting, punching, slapping, shoving, choking, biting, and restraining. However, the list also includes questions about other types of non-physical abuse. The list asks a woman, does your partner:

- constantly criticize you and your abilities as a spouse, parent, or employee?
- behave in an over-protective manner or become extremely jealous?
- threaten to hurt you, your children, pets, family members, friends, or himself?
- prevent you from seeing family or friends?
- get suddenly angry or lose his temper?
- destroy personal property or throw things around?
- deny you access to family assets like bank accounts, credit cards, or the car, or control all finances and force you to account for what you spend?
- force you to work in jobs not of your choosing?

- use intimidation or manipulation to control you or your children?
- prevent you from going where you want to, when you want to, and with whomever you want to?
- make you have sex when you don't want to or do things sexually that you don't want to do?
- humiliate or embarrass you in front of other people?[3]

In addition to physical abuse, these questions address emotional, psychological, social, and economic types of abuse. If a woman answers affirmatively to only one of these questions, she may be in an abusive relationship, and the root cause of her abuse may be a narcissistic husband.

In addition to this list that focuses on her husband's actions, a church leader or counselor can recognize that a woman is in an abusive relationship by considering her feelings and by asking questions such as the following:

- Are you anxious when you know he is about to walk in the door?
- Are you relieved when he is not around?
- Do you wish you could be anywhere he is not?
- Do you feel alone in your relationship with him because he is not emotionally available to you?

---

[3] These questions are posted on the website of the New York State Coalition Against Domestic Violence. Visit http://www.nyscadv.org.

- Are you emotionally drained and afraid to say or do anything because you do not know how he will respond?
- Do you fear him?
- Do you feel off-balance because you never know what kind of mood he will be in or what he may say or do?
- Are you constantly in crisis-mode?
- Do you feel put-down or humiliated by his words or actions?
- Do you feel that you are the butt of his jokes and that rather than laughing with you, he is laughing at you?
- Are you often confused because he has led you to believe one thing but later criticized you for holding such a "stupid" belief?
- Do you feel that you are never right about anything or that you can't do anything right?
- Do you feel minimized when he trivializes what you hold to be important or significant?
- Do you feel undermined or betrayed when he makes private information about you public?
- Do you feel powerless and helpless when you experience something unpleasant that he is saying or doing to you?
- Do you feel that you must justify, defend, or explain everything that you say or do?
- Do you feel that your life is out of your control?
- Do you feel isolated from family or friends because of him?

- Do you feel that you never have any money to spend on yourself or for the things you enjoy while he always seems to have money for his hobbies or the things he wants to do?

If a woman answers "Yes" to only a few of these questions, she may be in an abusive relationship.

When a woman and a pastoral counselor conclude that she's in such a relationship, several books and other resources offer some helpful strategies for responding to the situation.[4] If a woman's husband exhibits strong narcissistic tendencies, however, attempts to improve the situation are almost certainly doomed to failure.

When a woman really has tried everything she knows to do and continues to be undermined and devalued by her husband, what is she to do and how can her pastoral counselor responsibly advise her? Is divorce ever the best option for her?

A Pastor's Story

I was the pastor of a small church, and a lovely lady named Anne led the singing and supported the church in many other ways. She surprised me one day when she came into my office and informed me that she'd be leaving the church.

---

[4] See for example, Patricia Evans, *The Verbally Abusive Relationship: How to Recognize It and How to Respond* (Third Expanded Edition; Avon, MA: Adams Media Corporation, 2010).

Realizing the important role she played in the programs of our church, I asked her why she was leaving.

She explained, "I'm going to file for divorce. My husband has been abusive throughout our relationship, and I've reached the end of my road. I simply can't take it any longer. I know that God hates divorce and that the church doesn't approve of what I feel forced to do. Rather than embarrass you and the church, I've decided to leave the church."

Knowing that she was about to need me and the church during the difficulties of a divorce, I asked if she were open to exploring her decision. She responded affirmatively and so I continued. "You mentioned that God hates divorce, and indeed Malachi 2:16 does record that statement. Those who quote this biblical verse to prohibit divorce, however, rarely quote the entire passage. Let's just read it now." I took the Bible from my desk, and we read Malachi 2:14-16:

> The Lord was witness to the covenant between you and the wife of your youth, to whom you've been faithless, although she's your companion and your wife by covenant. Hasn't the one God made and sustained for us the spirit of life? What does he desire? Godly offspring. So look after yourselves, and let no one be faithless to the wife of his youth. "For I hate divorce," says the Lord the God of Israel, "and I hate covering one's garment with violence," says the Lord of hosts. Therefore look after yourselves and don't be faithless.

I explained that this passage relates to a time when the Jews had returned to their homeland from exile in Babylon. Some of the Jewish men were divorcing their Jewish wives to marry the daughters of wealthy non-Jewish landowners.[5]

Among other social injustices, Malachi judges this practice as "covering one's garment with violence." This passage does not state that God hates all divorce but only the divorce that perpetrates violence. This passage is silent about God's attitude toward a divorce that avoids or eliminates violence. The passage clearly asserts, however, that what God really hates is one spouse's treating the other with violence.

I then asked her, "Has your husband perpetrated violence on you?"

"Has he?" she answered with a quivering voice, "Only on a daily basis since almost the very beginning of our marriage."

She lowered her eyes, and I could see tears welling up. I calmly suggested, "Then perhaps, God doesn't hate divorce in your case since your decision to file for divorce is not to

---

[5] Catherine Clark Kroeger and Nancy Nason-Clark, *No Place for Abuse: Biblical and Practical Resources to Counteract Domestic Violence* (Downers Grove, IL: InterVarsity Press), 133. Another possible interpretation of the context of this passage is that these Jewish men were divorcing their foreign wives to comply with the strict marriage proclamations of Ezra 9:10-10:11 and Nehemiah 13:23-27 even though these women had been faithful to their marital vows. Even if this alternative interpretation is accepted, the fact that God hates the kind of divorce that violates a faithful partner remains the point this passage is making.

perpetrate violence but to prohibit it. I don't think the passage in Malachi really applies to your situation, and I don't think God hates divorce in your case. In fact, I think God is proud of you for filing for divorce since God didn't create you to be a verbal or emotional punching bag for anyone and you've decided to stand up for yourself and become what God intended you to be."

She raised her tear-filled eyes with a surprised look and asked, "How can God be proud of me for filing for divorce, when divorce is a sin?"

"Well now, I have trouble placing divorce in the category of sin," I said. "I haven't ever read a verse in the Bible that supports such an idea, and it's difficult for me to call divorce a sin since God is divorced but God has never sinned."

Her eyes grew wide with astonishment. "What do you mean God is divorced?" she asked.

"Well, God is," I responded, "according to the prophets Hosea and Jeremiah." I then explained that God commands Hosea to divorce his wife Gomer to exemplify God's divorce of faithless Israel. Hosea pronounces the ancient divorce formula to Gomer, "You're not my wife, and I'm not your husband" (Hosea 2:2).

Divorce at this time was swift and simple. The divorced wife had to leave her husband's house and was not permitted to return to her room or take anything but what she was wearing. This divorce practice explains why women in that society wore much gold and silver so that if a husband considered divorcing his wife he might think twice since a large portion of his wealth was about to walk out the door."

I continued, "This practice also explains why Moses commanded a husband to give his wife a written decree of divorce (Deuteronomy 24:1-4; Matthew 19:7; Mark 10:4). A devious husband might make the divorce pronouncement to his wife and later deny it and accuse her of adultery if she should marry another."

"Hosea is not being devious when he pronounces the divorce decree to Gomer. Instead, Hosea is following God's direction. Similar to Hosea, God pronounces the ancient divorce formula to Israel when God says, 'You're not my people, and I'm not your God' (Hosea 1:7; RSV). The prophet Jeremiah records God's explanation for divorcing Israel, 'For all the adulteries of that faithless one, Israel, I sent her away with a decree of divorce' (Jeremiah 3:8; RSV).

"Now if divorce were a sin," I asked, "how could God command Hosea to divorce Gomer and sin? Furthermore, how could God divorce Israel without sinning if divorce were a sin. Perhaps, now you understand why I have trouble calling divorce a sin."

"I never knew God was divorced," she said.

"Yes," I responded, "God is a divorcee, and God identifies with all those who experience the gut-wrenching, emotional roller coaster of a divorce. Just read the book of

Hosea and see how much pain God experiences in that divorce process. God indeed divorces an unfaithful marriage partner, but God does not sin."

"Well, I know Jesus permits divorce on the grounds of unfaithfulness," Anne said.

"Yes, but what constitutes unfaithfulness?" I asked.

"Adultery, of course," she answered.

"Yes, but unfaithfulness includes much more than adultery. In Matthew 19:3-9, Jesus was asked about the grounds for divorce. Let's read it. Maybe, I should first ask if you have time.

"Yes, I do," she reassured me.

"All right then," I said, "let's read the passage."

> Pharisees came up to Jesus and tested him by asking, "Is it lawful to divorce one's wife for any cause?" He responded, "Have you not read that he who made them from the beginning made them male and female, and said, 'For this reason a man shall leave his father and mother and be joined to his wife, and the two shall become one flesh.'? Thus, they're no longer two but one flesh. What therefore God has joined, let no man separate." The Pharisees said to Jesus, "Why then did Moses command a husband to give a certificate of divorce, and to put her away?" Jesus said to them, "For your hardness of heart Moses allowed you to divorce your wives, but from the beginning it was not so. I say to you, 'Whoever divorces his wife, except for a sexual indiscretion, and marries another, commits adultery.'"

"Anne, you're indeed correct," I said. "Jesus does permit divorce on the grounds of sexual infidelity."

"So then," she asserted, "I'm not permitted to get a divorce because Tom has never had an affair or been unfaithful to me with another woman."

"According to this passage alone, your conclusion is perhaps correct, but we need to consider what constitutes unfaithfulness and why Jesus was asked about divorce by these Pharisees."

I continued by explaining that the Pharisees are asking Jesus to comment on a hotly disputed verse in the Old Testament. The verse is Deuteronomy 24:1, which reads, "When a man takes a wife and marries her, if then she finds no favor in his eyes because he's found *some indecency* in her, he writes her a bill of divorce and puts it in her hand and sends her out of his house, and she departs out of his house."

"The problematic words in this passage are *some indecency.* The Hebrew words are ערבת דבר, which are best rendered as *an indecency of a matter.* The words would make more sense if they were reversed and read דבר ערבה, which is rendered as *a matter of indecency.*"

"Now, I certainly don't want to bore you with a Hebrew lesson," I said, "but these two words are very important because they occasioned a huge debate in Jesus' day about their meaning."[6]

I explained that the two prominent Pharisaical teachers were Shammai and Hillel. Both of these teachers founded houses or schools of interpretation. The House of Shammai restricted the meaning of these two words in Deuteronomy 24:1 to adultery. The House of Hillel held their meaning to refer to any defect or anything displeasing that a husband found in his wife.

The Pharisees who asked Jesus about divorce were probably from the House of Hillel because they ask if it's lawful for a man to divorce his wife *for any cause* (Matthew 19:3). This position of *divorce for any cause* was held by the House of Hillel.

Jesus' unequivocal answer is that these two Hebrew words refer only to sexual infidelity (Matthew 19:9). In other words, Jesus sides with the House of Shammai on the interpretation of Deuteronomy 24:1. Jesus does not understand this verse as permitting divorce for any cause or reason but only for adultery or some other sexual indiscretion.

Many who read this encounter between Jesus and these Pharisees over the correct interpretation of Deuteronomy 24:1,

---

[6] A summary of this debate can be found in David Instone-Brewer, *Divorce and Remarriage in the Bible: The Social and Literary Context* (Grand Rapids: Eerdmans, 2002), 100-114.

prematurely conclude that Jesus' interpretation of this one verse comprises Jesus complete understanding of divorce and the grounds on which a divorce may be legitimately pursued. Such is not the case, however. Jesus was only asked to comment on his interpretation of Deuteronomy 24:1 because this verse was the only divorce text in the Old Testament that was in dispute in Jesus' day.

"Am I boring you with too much detail?" I asked. "I know I've a tendency to do that."

"No, no, no," Anne responded, "I'm finding all this very fascinating."

"Okay, then." As I was saying, "There was another divorce text that was very important in Jesus' day, but it was not in dispute and Jesus was not asked to interpret it because everyone agreed on its interpretation. This text is Exodus 21:10-11, which reads, 'If he takes another wife to himself, he shall not decrease his first wife's food, her clothing, or her marital rights. If he does not do these three things for her, she shall go out free, without payment of money.'"

I explained, "Everyone in Jesus' day including Jesus as well interpreted these verses as permitting a woman to divorce her husband if he didn't provide her with food, clothing, and marital rights. The notion of marital rights is rather broad and included whatever a wife has a right to expect from her husband.[7] Her expectations would of course include protection but she also has a right to be loved, honored, and cherished. All these things are expressed in the marriage vows you and Tom exchanged."

At this point she interrupted with some emotion in her voice, "He certainly hasn't lived up to his end of our vows then. His constant abusive behavior has made me feel anything but loved, honored, and cherished. And protection, ha, I need to be protected from him more than from anyone or anything else."

"Help me understand," I said, "You mean that he hasn't provided you with what a wife has a right to expect from her husband?"

"Absolutely, not," she quickly shot back.

"Then, even though Deuteronomy 24:1 doesn't permit you to file for divorce," I said, "you nevertheless have grounds to divorce Tom on the basis of Exodus 21:10-11. He's been unfaithful to you by not providing what he vowed on the day you were married."

"Do you think Jesus would agree?" she asked.

"I'm certain that he would unless he disagreed with every other Jew in the first century," I responded. "Jesus certainly didn't hesitate to disagree with others. If he disagreed with

---

[7] The meaning of the Hebrew word עֹנָתָהּ is disputed, but it probably refers to whatever a wife has a right to expect from her husband such as being loved, honored, and cherished. See the discussion of its meaning in Instone-Brewer, *Divorce and Remarriage*, 100.

these Pharisees about the interpretation of Exodus 21:10-11, I expect he would've taken the opportunity when these Pharisees asked him about divorce to set them straight not only on Deuteronomy 24:1 but also on Exodus 21:10-11."

I continued, "Since he didn't, I'm convinced that Jesus interpreted the divorce text in Exodus as every other Jew in the first century and included a husband's failure to provide food, clothing, and what a wife has a right to expect from her husband along with adultery as biblical grounds for divorce."[8]

"Oh my!" Anne said, "I never knew."

"Well, now that you know," I said, "I hope you'll reconsider your decision to leave our church. I'll stand with you during your divorce."

"Tom is going to be so surprised," she said.

"What do you mean?" I asked.

"When I approached him about filing for divorce," she responded, "he asked how I could divorce him when the Bible, the church, and God were against it. I know Tom is expecting you to be on his side and to try and convince me not to file for divorce."

"Well, he is indeed in for a surprise," I said, "because I'm not going to try and convince you not to file. As a matter of fact, I'll accompany you to see a lawyer if you want."

"What are you going to say to Tom?" she asked.

---

[8] Instone-Brewer, *Divorce and Remarriage*, 286.

"Well, I'll tell him that he's the one who broke his marriage vows with you by treating you as his personal verbal and emotional punching bag and that there's no reason for you to hold up your end of the marriage vows when he's failed so miserably in holding up his end."

"I'll tell him that he abdicated his role as your husband the moment he began verbally and emotionally abusing you and that all you're doing by filing for divorce is legally recognizing what he's already done. I think he'll get an ear full if I have the opportunity to speak with him."

"My, my," Anne said, "I'm glad I stopped by to see you today."

"So am I," I responded.

"May I ask you one further question that troubles me?" she inquired.

"Certainly," I said.

"What about remarriage? If I divorce Tom, may I remarry or must I remain single for the rest of my life? I recall somewhere Jesus' saying that if a woman divorces her husband and marries another, she commits adultery. After our discussion this afternoon, I now understand that divorce is not a sin and is permitted in my situation, but it seems remarriage is a problem and wouldn't be an option for me. It scares me to think that I'll have to spend the rest of my life alone."

"You've a very good memory," I said, "and the passage you mention is Mark 10:11-12, which reads, "Whoever divorces his wife and marries another woman, commits adultery against her; and if she divorces her husband and marries another man, she commits adultery." This passage occurs in Mark's version of the Pharisees' asking Jesus about divorce in Deuteronomy 24:1 and should be understood along with Matthew's version of their question.

According to Matthew 19:9, Jesus answers the Pharisees and says, "Whoever divorces his wife, except for sexual unfaithfulness, and marries another, commits adultery." Although not in Mark's version, Matthew's version adds "except for sexual unfaithfulness." On the basis of Deuteronomy 24:1, Jesus' statement according to Matthew's version permits remarriage after divorce if the other partner has been sexually unfaithful."

"The other divorce text in Exodus 21:10-11 also permits remarriage after divorce for other types of unfaithfulness when it states that the defrauded wife 'shall be given her freedom absolutely.' She is free to remarry. Even though he hasn't committed adultery, Tom's unfaithfulness to you in these other areas gives you biblical grounds for marrying someone else after your divorce."

I quickly added, "I'd caution you, however, to be very careful here. I've seen so many women escape from one abusive relationship only to land quickly in another. You need to take time after your divorce to find out about yourself."

"What was it about you that attracted you to an abuser in the first place? Do you have healthy and clear boundaries that you enforce? Unless you find out about yourself and gain some insight into your own relational dynamics, you'll likely end up with another Tom."

She thought for a moment and then said, "I've learned a lot about myself in the many years I've spent with Tom, but I know I still have much to learn, and I definitely don't want to end up in another relationship like this one. If I ever decide to remarry, I'll carefully consider what you've just said." Then she asked, "Would you be willing to help me work through some of my issues?"

"Yes, but you may also want to consider the services of a professional counselor as well," I answered.

"Okay, I know I've taken a lot of your time this afternoon," Anne said, "but may I ask you just one last question?"

"Sure," I quickly answered.

"What about the church? Will the church stand by me and support my decision to file for divorce?"

"I don't know for certain," I cautiously answered. "Many hold different views in our church. I can't speak for the church, but I can tell you that I'll preach and teach the biblical passages as we've discussed them today. We can only hope that the church will hear and understand these passages and stand with you and support you in seeking a divorce."

Wise as Serpents and Harmless as Doves

Jesus calls his followers and the church to be wise as serpents and harmless as doves. Unless Jesus' followers and the church wise up to narcissism, it's unlikely they'll be harmless as doves. The harm that well-meaning followers of Jesus and the church have already done by encouraging and even forcing women to remain in toxic narcissistic relationships is enormous.

Narcissistic husbands are so effective at recruiting others that often the church has stood with them against their victimized wives. The church's prohibition on divorce has frequently kept these women locked in the torture chamber of the narcissist's manipulation and control. Too many times, narcissistic husbands have used the church and the Bible as clubs to beat their wives into subservience.

Being wise as serpents means that the followers and the church of Jesus will no longer be ignorant of the toxic effects of narcissism and the devious, manipulative tactics of narcissistic husbands. Being harmless as doves means the church will no longer stand guard at the door of a woman's torture chamber but rather will break down that door and usher her to freedom from the narcissistic imposter who projects himself as her husband.

Chapter 5
Hope for Change and Expectation of a Miracle

In addition to the biblical teachings about male headship, female submission, and the church's prohibition against divorce, the biblical suggestion for the wife to expect a miraculous change in her husband as a result of her patient suffering often preserves toxic narcissistic relationships.[1] Both biblical texts that discuss this possibility talk about believing wives married to husbands outside the faith community.

1 Peter 3:1-2 suggests to these wives that unbelieving husbands "may be won apart from a word through the behavior of their wives as they look upon your chaste, reverent behavior." The Apostle Paul asks, "Wife, how do you know whether you'll save your husband" (1 Corinthians 7:16)? Holding out hope for a miraculous change in her narcissistic husband has kept many women locked in his torture chamber as she languishes in the toxic relationship his narcissism creates.

Is it possible for a narcissistic husband to change and to modify his behavior to remove the toxicity from his marriage?

---

[1] For a discussion of this topic, see Catherine Clark Kroeger and Nancy Nason-Clark, *No Place for Abuse: Biblical and Practical Resources to Counteract Domestic Violence* (Downers Grove, IL: InterVarsity Press, 2001), 91-99. Chapter 7 of this book is entitled, "Does the Suffering of an Abused Woman Bring Salvation to Her Husband? *First Peter Revisited.*"

Hollywood thinks so. Jean Twenge and Keith Campbell observe that many movies present the miraculous cure of a narcissist.[2] Hypnosis (*Shallow Hal*), electric shock (*What Women Want*), future revelations (*A Christmas Carol*), repeating the same day over and over (*Groundhog Day*), and being shot in the head (*Regarding Henry*) are all means Hollywood uses to portray the miraculous cure of a narcissist. Are these means really effective in curing narcissism? Twenge and Campbell and other psychologists certainly don't think so.

A woman's voice:

"My marriage was a disaster. He was so verbally and emotionally abusive that I could hardly stand to be around him. When his abuse turned to violence, I became truly frightened for my life and sought advice from a pastor. He told me that I should stay with my husband and model the Christian life for him. This pastor said that I should pray for my husband's conversion and that God would use my life to save my husband. I wasn't certain this pastor's advice was sound so I sought out another pastor who advised me to leave my husband. This pastor explained that God never intended for anyone to be a punching bag for someone else and that I could pray for my husband from afar just as well as while living with him. I decided to follow the first pastor's advice since I was determined not to fail in my marriage. Seven more years I lived with the horrible abuse with no change. After I unexpectedly became pregnant and gave birth to my daughter, I decided the second pastor was right after all. I could no longer tolerate the abuse, and I certainly couldn't subject my little daughter to the violent, angry outbursts of my husband. I regret I wasted those seven years with a disappointed hope he'd change."

---

[2] Jean M. Twenge and W. Keith Campbell, *The Narcissism Epidemic: Living in the Age of Entitlement* (New York: Free Press, 2009), 280.

One counselor explains the hopelessness of therapy for narcissists. He states that very few narcissists will ever agree to participate in counseling because nothing is ever their fault and they have no defects that need addressing. Nevertheless, under the threat of divorce or the loss of their children, some narcissists find their way into his office.

This counselor has developed a special therapy to treat narcissists. This therapy concentrates on the development of empathy. Despite his specialized empathy therapy, this counselor reports that he's able to help only about 2% of the narcissists he sees. That's only one in fifty. This counselor is very emphatic that he's not able to cure this one but only able to help him modify his behavior to improve his relationships somewhat. The other 49 are resistant to change. Other counselors report a similarly disappointing success rate. Narcissism resists even skilled and professional therapists.

Sam Vaknin confirms these counselors' assessment about the difficulty of curing a narcissist. Vaknin explains that he's not a psychiatrist and that his educational training is not what enabled him to write his book on narcissism. Instead, he admits that he's a narcissist and his personality disorder along with the loss of his family, career, and reputation is what prompted him to write his book. He explains that his book documents "a road of self-discovery" and that the process was painful, but "led to nowhere." Even though he spent numerous hours in counseling and even though he wrote his book on narcissism, he confesses that he remains unchanged and that his "disorder is here to stay." He concludes that the prognosis for his recovery is poor and alarming.[3]

Vaknin's self-disclosure is chilling and discouraging. He's the rare narcissist who finally faces into his disorder and even realizes that the failures in his life are his fault. Nevertheless, his recovery "led to nowhere," and he offers little hope for a cure. The overwhelming prognosis of Vaknin and many who work with narcissists is that the narcissist probably won't change.[4]

Given this dismal prognosis for the cure of a narcissistic husband, the question must be asked if the Bible offers false hope to the wives of narcissists. One way to answer this question is of course, "Yes." This answer, however, is inconsistent with the otherwise practical and truthful message of the Bible.

Another more consistent way is to answer "No, since God's transforming power far exceeds the abilities of human counselors." God most certainly does have the power to change a narcissistic husband. Nevertheless, God created humans with

---

[3] Sam Vaknin, *Malignant Self Love: Narcissism Revisited* (Prague & Skopje: Narcissus Publications, 2003), 15.

[4] Vaknin's approach to narcissism is psychodynamic. Behavioral psychologists are more optimistic about "quieting the ego" of the narcissist. For example, see Twenge and Campbell, *The Narcissism Epidemic*, 282-286.

free will and respects that free will. For a narcissist to be forgiven and reconciled to God, the narcissist must genuinely repent and accept responsibility for his sins. Such an admission is virtually impossible for a narcissist since it would destroy the false image that is reality for him.

The prospect of losing his entire sense of self that he's worked so hard to project and maintain is so threatening for the narcissist that he won't likely do what it takes to access God's transforming power. Even though many narcissists attend church because they see the church as a powerful manipulative tool and image-enhancer, they nevertheless resist the transforming power of the church's message.

So does the Bible offer false hope to the wives of narcissists? The best answer is "No, since the Bible doesn't include narcissistic husbands when discussing husbands who may be won by their wives' behavior."

One indication that this explanation is preferable is Paul's statement that a believing wife isn't bound if her unbelieving husband decides to leave her, "for God has indeed called us to peace" (1 Corinthians 7:15). Since a woman's relationship with a narcissistic husband is rarely peaceful, Paul must not be including narcissistic husbands among those who may be won by their wives' remaining in the relationship. Thus, the Bible doesn't offer women false hope that they may win their husbands by their suffering and chaste behavior because the

Bible doesn't include narcissistic husbands among this potential group of converts.

The final guard at the door of her torture chamber is now removed, and a woman no longer needs to remain in a toxic narcissistic relationship by expecting a miraculous change in her husband by her suffering. Such wishful thinking actually plays into the hands of her controlling narcissistic husband. He probably won't change, and the sooner she stops trying to change him, the more time and energy she'll have to devote to her own development and productivity.

Les Carter, a counselor who specializes in narcissism, explains, "Although it may seem unfair that those bearing the brunt of the negative narcissistic behavior should have to be the ones to change or adapt, the truth is that they are the only ones in the relationship who can change the dynamics."[5] If a woman decides to stay with a narcissistic husband, she must be the one to change because he probably never will.

Although all the guards at the door of her torture chamber have now been removed and she's free to escape and leave the toxic relationship with him, she may choose to stay for a variety of reasons, and Part 3 explains the survival strategies she'll need to stay.

---

[5] Les Carter, *Enough about You, Let's Talk about Me: How to Recognize and Manage the Narcissists in Your Life* (San Francisco: Jossey-Bass A Wiley Imprint, 2005), viii.

Part 3

Making the Narcissistic Recipe Less Toxic

Chapter 6
Choosing to Stay

Although biblical divorce texts such as Exodus 21:10-11 give a woman the right to leave a husband who doesn't fulfill his vows to her, these texts don't require a woman to leave. She's free to leave, but she may decide to stay in the marriage for a variety of reasons.

One of the primary reasons both for staying and for leaving is children. Divorce is hard on adults but in many ways harder on children. A woman with legitimate grounds for divorce must carefully weigh the effects of a divorce on her children with the prospects for remaining in the marriage. Sometimes remaining is better for the children, but more often than not taking the children out of a failed marriage is the better option especially if her husband is narcissistic.

As devastating as his narcissism is for her, it's far more devastating on her children. If a woman decides to stay in a marriage with a narcissistic husband, she should read some books such as *Children of the Self-Absorbed* and *The Narcissistic Family.*[1] She needs to know how to counteract as

---

[1] Nina W. Brown, *Children of the Self-Absorbed: A Grownup's Guide to Getting over Narcissistic Parents* (Oakland, CA: New Harbinger's Publications, Inc., 2001) and Stephanie Donaldson-Pressman and Robert M. Pressman, *The Narcissistic Family: Diagnosis and Treatment* (San Francisco: Jossey-Bass, 1994).

much as possible the damage his narcissism is likely to cause for them. A woman who decides to remain in a toxic narcissistic relationship also needs to develop some strategies to protect herself and her children from him.

A woman's voice:

"My teenage daughter went to visit her father just after she'd completed a school project. She was proud of her project, and so was I. She'd worked very, very hard and had put her soul into her project. I was anxious to know what her father thought about it, and when she returned from her visit I asked her what his response was. 'Oh,' she said, 'I didn't even take my project with me to show him because I knew he would have so much to tell me about his life, his accomplishments, and his experiences that he wouldn't really notice mine anyway.' That hurt just to think that my daughter knew him so well that she wouldn't even try to share her accomplishment with him. She knew his soul well, but he was so full of himself that he could never know hers."

A Mother's Story

My daughter dropped by one Saturday afternoon to help me bake some pies and other desserts for Thanksgiving Dinner. After we put the pies in the oven, we decided to sit down and take a well-deserved break. As we sipped hot tea and sampled some of the other desserts we'd made, my daughter began to talk about her marriage to Ted.

At first I was glad because she'd become more secretive and distant from me since she married him. I'd often wondered about their relationship and if she were happy. My gladness, however, turned to a chilling sadness when she said to me, "Mom, I think I married someone just like dad."

"Oh, no!" I recoiled in myself and dropped my head into my hands. I'd often suspected that Ted was a lot like Dick, but when that thought crossed my mind, I banished it as quickly as I could. I could hardly bear the thought of my daughter's enduring the pain and suffering I'd endured in my 27 years of marriage to Dick.

My daughter continued, "Mom, how have you done it? I know how difficult dad is, and I remember the fighting and arguing you and he used to do. What did you do to change him?"

I raised my head from my hands and said, "Change him? No way. It was bad in the early years of our marriage."

My daughter interrupted, "It's pretty bad in my marriage too, mom."

My heart sank, and I reached over and took her hand in mine. Our eyes met, and there was an exchange of understanding that can only occur between two people who have been pushed to the edge by extreme suffering.

"It was even worse than bad," I continued. "The more I tried to engage your dad and ask him to meet me half way, the worse it became. I became so depressed that I felt my very self was being crushed beneath a huge boulder. I could hardly breathe. He was like an enormous weight pressing down on me and squeezing the very life out of me. When I tried to talk to him about my feelings, he only increased the pressure."

"Wow! Mom, Ted is a lot like dad," she commented. "So what did you do?" she asked.

"Well, one day when I was in complete despair and at the end of my rope, I sat myself down and reflected on my situation. I finally admitted that I was never going to be able to change your dad and that I should stop wasting my time trying.

Instead, I decided to try to improve my situation by changing the only person I could, myself. I decided that I had to act differently in our relationship if my marriage, but more importantly, if I were going to survive. I tried a lot of things over the next few years and took many different approaches. Some worked; some didn't. What worked, I kept doing; what didn't, I dropped."

"Mom," she said, "that is what I really need to know. What worked?" she asked expectantly.

I thought for a moment and then said, "I believe there were at least four basic things I changed about myself that have helped me. I learned in any given instance to focus on the task at hand, to stick to the facts, to pull back my emotions, and to establish my boundaries."

"Focus on the task at hand, stick to the facts, pull back emotions, establish boundaries," my daughter repeated trying to fix them in her memory. "So how do each of these things work, mom?" she asked.

Again, I thought for a moment and then replied, "An example," I said, "may be the best way for me to explain how these things have worked in my interactions with your dad. Let's just say that one evening I was in the kitchen when your dad walked in and asked what I was doing. I reply, 'I'm cooking dinner.'

He quickly snaps back, 'Well, I hope you do a better job than you usually do. You're cooking is terrible.'

He knows how much I pride myself in my cooking. What he's trying to do is to get an emotional response from me. He gets some strange satisfaction by drawing an emotional rise out of me. In the early years of our marriage, I'd respond angrily, 'That's not true. I'm an excellent cook.' A heated argument would follow. I'd feel as if I were in a competition with him about who had the right to judge my cooking. I'd usually end up crying and he'd have gotten what he wanted, an emotional reaction from me. I rarely won any of these arguments with him since he prided himself on always being right. No matter how much I argued, I couldn't change his mind."

"Mom," my daughter said, "I could give you several similar examples from my encounters with Ted. So how did you learn to respond differently?" she asked.

"I learned that instead of responding in that way with an angry emotional outburst, I had to pull back my emotions and stick to the facts by calmly saying, 'That's your opinion.' I'd made a factual statement and he really couldn't argue with it. It was his opinion that my cooking was terrible.

At first, he'd continue trying to draw me into an emotional argument by saying, 'No, that's everyone's opinion. No one thinks you're a good cook.'

He knew how much I cared about what others thought, and he was just trying to push my buttons."

"How did you respond to that, mom," she asked.

"I calmly said to him, 'That's your perception about what everyone else thinks.' Again, I'd made a factual statement without agreeing with his assessment of my cooking or how everyone else thinks about it. I'd preserved my sense of self and my right to decide the quality of my cooking. I'd even remind myself of all the numerous awards I'd received for my cooking, but I didn't dare mention them to him. He'd just use this fact to berate the judges at those cooking contests to demonstrate his superiority to them and assert that he, not they, had the correct view about my cooking. After pulling back my emotions and sticking to the facts, I just continued focusing on the task at hand and kept on preparing dinner."

"Mom, that sounds like a really good approach, but I don't think Ted will give up so easily."

"In the beginning, your dad didn't give up so easily either," I said. "I had to establish a boundary to protect myself from his unceasing tirade about my cooking. I realized that allowing him to continue his tirade and to make me listen to his repeated negative comments made me feel powerless and emboldened his sense of control over me. I guess he thought that even if he couldn't draw me into an emotional argument or get me to accept his point of view, he could force me to listen to his cutting words."

"I came to realize that I didn't have to listen to his criticisms and that I had power over my own hearing. Just like a radio or television that says things I don't want to hear, I could tune him out. So, I'd set my boundary and say, 'If you continue criticizing my cooking, I'll stop.' If he didn't respect my boundary but continued his tirade, I'd enforce my boundary by leaving the kitchen and going outside or to the mall or anywhere else where his words couldn't reach me."

"He had to manage his own dinners a few times. Each time, he raged at me, but each time I just focused on the task at hand, stuck to the facts, pulled back my emotions, and set and defended my boundaries. Nothing ever changed in him, but over time, I began to feel better about myself and my situation by changing myself."

"Mom, this sounds like really good advice. I can't wait to start using it in my encounters with Ted."

"Well, don't be too hard on yourself if you falter somewhat at first," I said. "It does take practice and determination, and you must remember that your goal isn't to change Ted but to enable yourself just to survive his antics." Just then the timer buzzed, and our pies were ready to take from the oven. I just hoped my daughter was really ready to do what it was going to take to live with someone like Ted, someone like my husband.

Strategies for Staying with a Narcissistic Husband

If you're married to someone with narcissistic personality traits and you decide to remain with him, you'll need to perfect the strategies of focusing on the task at hand, sticking to the facts, pulling back your emotions, and then setting and enforcing your boundaries.

Focus on the Task at Hand

Focusing on the task at hand is important when interacting with a narcissist. Narcissists are not about tasks but about securing narcissistic supply to sustain the projection of their false self. The narcissist cares more about *image* than *substance*, and you must realize that your goals to get things done will never coincide with his goal to reaffirm his illusory image of himself.

To avoid allowing him to side-track you and co-opt you for his agenda, you must set your own agenda and stick to it. At any given moment, you need to focus on the task at hand. At the end of the day, you may feel completely worn out, used up, or completely drained with little to show for your efforts. In narcissistic marriages, many tasks usually remain undone as energy and resources are constantly consumed to maintain his image. Unless you focus on the task at hand, you'll likely experience constant frustration and feel overwhelmed as undone tasks pile up on you.

Making a daily list of the tasks you want to accomplish is one effective way for you to avoid the dissipating antics of your husband. A list enables you to focus on what you think really needs to be done. You should be aware that he'll likely make every effort to thwart your agenda and may even ridicule your list and shame you for being enslaved to it. You need to remember that it's better to be bound to a list than to be enslaved to him.

When he tries to side-track you or throw you off balance by bringing up other tasks that he wants done, you can say to him, "That's not on my list for today. If you feel that task is important, then take care of it yourself." Such a response may seem unnatural to you, for you probably entered marriage thinking that marriage is give-and-take.

The problem with that kind of thinking is that for the narcissist, the give is always from you and the take is always for him. Admittedly, your singular focus on your list is an unnatural and restrictive way to live, but it's an effective way to live with a narcissistic husband unless you want to stop living and turn your life over to him.

Stick to Facts

As you focus on the task at hand, you must stick to facts if you're to retain your balance and your reality. The narcissist creates his own reality by selecting some facts that support his illusion, denying others that challenge it, and fabricating still many others that he feels he needs to maintain it.

Your narcissistic husband may have the uncanny ability to create self-doubt and uncertainty in you. By constantly challenging your view of reality and making you defend every perception you have, he may try to wear you down and substitute his set of fabricated facts with your real ones.

You can only resist being drawn into his insane world by sticking firmly to your own set of facts. Since he's so good at what he does, you may need to seek professional help or at least a friend or family member to help you. You need someone with whom you can discuss your facts and receive confirmation that you're indeed not off base in your assessments.

One effective way you can stick to facts is to close your ears in the presence of your narcissistic husband and open your eyes. No matter what he says about why he deserves new clothes even though you haven't bought any for months, you need to open your eyes and see that his closet is filled with nice clothes while your wardrobe is perhaps a bit scanty. No matter what he says about how well he provides for you, close your ears and open your eyes to see that he buys the best of everything for himself while garage sales and second hand stores are good enough for you.

No matter what he says about your poor mothering skills, you need to open your eyes and see that your children are well-cared for. No matter what he says about your failings as a wife, close your ears and open your eyes to see all that you're doing for the marriage. No matter what he says about your emotional state, you need to open your eyes and see that he's the one who's behaving strangely. By closing your ears, you can shut out his efforts to get you off balance. By opening your eyes, you can see that your set of facts is far more realistic and accurate than his.

A woman's voice:

"My husband was a prominent member of our church and community. He had time and energy for everyone except for me and the kids. Worse than that, he was a terror at home. I tried to talk with my pastor and a few others but finally gave up. They just couldn't believe the husband and father I was describing was the wonderful man they knew. With everyone else so convinced of his goodness, I doubted myself and wondered what was wrong with me. In the midst of the insanity of all those years, I couldn't deny one fact. He undermined me and the kids and treated us horribly. I finally could take it no longer and filed for divorce. He was so angry that I had tarnished his image in the eyes of our church and community. His family was disintegrating before his very eyes and all he was concerned about was his image. His final act almost pushed me over the edge and has made it very difficult for me. He committed suicide and left a note that named me and simply read, 'It's all your fault!' It has taken many hours of therapy for me to realize that his final act of cruelty was his own decision. I now know the truth , and it was not my fault."

Pull Back Emotions

Perhaps the hardest strategy to follow when dealing with a narcissist is to pull back emotions, especially for a woman and wife. The narcissist devotes his entire time and energies to eliciting an emotional response from her to make himself feel and look good. When narcissists don't get the narcissistic supply they crave, they're like bees separated from their hive. They continue to swarm around and try everything to realize their desires. A narcissistic husband often drives his wife first to frustration, then to anger and fear, and finally to hopelessness. If she capitulates and expresses her emotions to him, he'll be back again and again to feed on the narcissistic supply she's giving to him.

Pulling back emotions is not the same as denying emotions. You will of course feel various emotions, and you need to name them and own them for yourself. If you don't name and accept the emotions you're feeling, you may become depressed, for you're denying an important part of yourself. You should be in touch with your own emotions.

However, you need to be careful expressing them to him. In the very moment that you let go and permit your tone of voice or your body language to express your emotions to him, he'll likely use and manipulate them to hook you and to extract his narcissistic supply. You must guard your emotions every time you speak or interact with him.

Once you pull back your emotions, he'll usually accuse you of becoming cold toward him. He may say, "What has happened? You're so cold." Since marriage is supposed to provide emotional warmth, he wants you to feel as though you're failing as a wife. You need to realize that you're not failing, for you could never supply enough emotional energy or narcissistic supply to satisfy him even if you try by becoming emotionally exhausted yourself.

Once he realizes that you're no longer going to be a source of narcissistic supply for him, he'll probably seek it elsewhere. At this point, he may turn to other family members or co-workers. He may even have an affair or multiple ones. Whatever he does, you must realize that he's making the choices he's making and that you're not to blame. He's the one who refuses to come to grips with his over-inflated self and his excessive self-admiration as well as his unrealistic expectation for narcissistic supply from you.

It may seem unnatural and abnormal for you to pull back your emotions, and it is, but you need to if you're going to survive his narcissistic abnormality. Be careful about giving in to your natural instinct to share your emotions and your feelings with him. If you haven't learned already, you need to be aware that a narcissist can't be trusted with your emotions but will instead habitually use them to make himself feel better about himself, often at your expense. After all, his entire existence is all about himself, not about you.

A woman's voice:

"My husband had just worn me out over the years until I had nothing left to give. He has so often made me mad and angry that I eventually just stopped caring. It was shortly after that when he first brought her into our home. He said she was going through a rough period in her life and needed our help. At first, I agreed since I really like to help people although I hadn't had much time or energy to do that since becoming his wife. One day as they were lying on our bed and watching television while I was in the kitchen preparing a meal, I looked around and said to myself, 'What is wrong with this picture.' My husband had forced me to become the maid in my own home while he courted another wife in the bedroom. When I walked into the bedroom to confront him about this, they were doing more than just lying there. . . ."

Set and Enforce Boundaries

Setting and enforcing boundaries are absolutely necessary for effective interaction with a narcissist since a narcissist knows no boundaries between himself and the rest of his world. He perceives the entire world as an extension of himself and everything and everyone in it are put there to meet his every whimsical desire.

When someone establishes a boundary, the narcissist typically makes it his sworn duty to cross over it and violate it by every means possible. He sees crossing others' boundaries as confirmation of his prowess and power. He won't rest until he has obliterated even the most personal boundaries of someone caught in his sights. Only by setting and enforcing clear boundaries can the wife of a narcissistic husband survive his constant attempts to violate her.

A woman's voice:

"Seven months after we were married, we moved a short distance away from our families to a nearby community. I was told by my husband Jason that we needed a fresh start and to be by ourselves. Shortly after we moved in, I was excited and happy about some happening at school that day and wanted to share it with Jason. I bounded up the stairs to the office room. As I rounded the corner, the image on the computer screen in front of him was horrifying. I may have been, as some would say, "sheltered", but in my 19 years I'd never seen or been exposed to pornography. My heart sank deeply into the pit of my stomach and I began to sweat. As Jason was fumbling around the keyboard and trying to click the image off, he realized that I'd already seen what he'd been doing.

I don't really remember the conversations in those moments right afterward, but they did include phrases such as, 'It was the first time I've looked...' or 'it just popped up on the screen and I couldn't get it off,' and 'You know no one loves you more than me.' The days following, I was devastated. Up to that point, I thought I was the only one he could ever want. Silence was my way of dealing with the pain until my first day back at work. I worked for my father-in-law at the time. He realized something was very wrong and badgered me until I told him what was upsetting me. After I told him what I'd seen, he laughed and said, 'Oh, is that all?' His laughter rang in my ears and my heart broke again as I felt worthless, misunderstood, depressed and very much alone.

Needless to say, I didn't want any physical touch from Jason during this time. I needed time to figure out my feelings. However, he was ready to 'prove' how much he loved me despite the pornography. He thought sex was a way to show me or 'prove' how much he loved me. After many times of his trying to initiate sex and my turning him down, he'd wait no more. Staring at the ceiling, tears streaming down the sides of my face, with my youth and innocence gone, I lay still and silent while he 'proved' how much he loved me."

Boundary setting and enforcing may be particularly difficult for you if you're married to a narcissist. Lack of clear boundaries is probably one of the reasons he targeted you in the first place.

Boundaries require a definite sense of self, and the wife of a narcissist often has a trampled sense of self. Instead of helping her to develop fixed boundaries of what she'd accept and tolerate in life and what she wouldn't, a domineering or narcissistic parent constantly caused her to question her natural boundaries and ran rough shod over them.

Our bodies provide a natural boundary between ourselves and the rest of the world. In childhood, however, the wife of a narcissistic husband probably had this boundary violated over and over again. At the dinner table when she announced that she was finished and wanted nothing else to eat, her parent or parents pressured her to take one more bite or to eat her carrots or something else.

They challenged her boundary instead of confirming it by saying to her, "You've the right to choose how much you eat and if you're full and want to stop eating." They may even violate her boundary by saying to her, "You can't get down from the dinner table until you've eaten some more." Such treatment conditions her to accept crossings of her boundaries as "normal." When she meets her narcissistic husband-to-be, she doesn't recognize the danger signals of his boundary violations, but accepts them as natural.

If you're married to a narcissist, learning to set real boundaries is thus perhaps difficult for you and enforcing them is probably even harder. However, you must if you're going to survive your life with a narcissistic husband. You need to realize that a real boundary must have a consequence if it's violated. Lack of a consequence demonstrates that the boundary was not actually a real one. If you say, "I won't talk with someone who yells at me," but do nothing when he continues yelling, you haven't established a real boundary.

You must convince your narcissistic husband that his violations of your boundaries will always definitely result in a consequence, usually one that he doesn't prefer. When you say that you won't talk with someone who's yelling, you need to add, "And I'll go somewhere else if you continue yelling." The very next time he yells, you need to stop talking and exit the situation by going shopping or to a friend's house or just anywhere he's not. Only by setting and enforcing real boundaries can you survive his attempts to violate your boundaries.

Establishing and enforcing boundaries are usually so difficult for the wife of a narcissist that you'll likely need help. Reading a few good books on boundaries is a good idea. Many books on boundaries have appeared recently, and three are really helpful.

The first two are by Anne Katherine and are entitled *Boundaries: Where You End and I Begin* (New York: Simon and Schuster, 1993) and *Where to Draw the Line: How to Set Healthy Boundaries Every Day* (New York: Simon and Schuster, 2000).

The third book is by Henry Cloud and John Townsend and is entitled *Boundaries: When to Say Yes, When to Say No to Take Control of Your Life* (Grand Rapids: Zondervan, 1992). These books are essential reading not only for you if you decide to stay with your narcissistic husband but also for you if you decide to leave since healthy boundaries will help prevent you from falling for or being recruited by another narcissist.

Living with a narcissistic husband is perhaps one of the most difficult things any human ever does, and your decision to stay with him is never going to be an easy one. As you have already read in this book, you're indeed free to leave. If you should decide to stay, however, you'll do well to focus on the task at hand, stick to facts, pull back your emotions, and then set and defend your boundaries.

Most importantly, however, you must always have a plan of escape if you feel your safety is threatened by him. Find out about local shelters for abused women and other resources and protective services you may need to make your escape. Deciding to stay is always difficult, but when it becomes dangerous to stay, you must be prepared to leave at a moment's notice if you or your children's safety is ever at risk.

Conclusion

In the pages of this book, you've read a Bible story that portrayed a toxic, narcissistic marriage. You've also read the stories of a stranger, a father, a sister, a pastor, and a mother. Perhaps, you've recognized yourself in one of these supporting roles, and someone you love is trapped in one of these toxic marriages. Hopefully, you now have a better idea of what your loved one is facing in her marriage to a narcissistic husband. Hopefully, reading this book enables you to help her cope and survive or even perhaps leave her toxic narcissistic husband.

If while reading this book, you've sadly recognized yourself more in the text boxes and have identified with the women's voices from the narcissistic torture chambers, you should now realize you're not alone and that there's really nothing wrong with you beyond what is normal for us as humans.

Maybe, you can now realize there's something seriously wrong with your narcissistic husband. Ideally, you feel empowered to let him no longer enslave you with his unfounded claim of superiority as your head or to dominate you with his false insistence on your subservience to him. Now that you have read this book, you should realize that divorce is indeed an option for you and that nothing is really forcing you to remain in his torture chamber.

Even if you decide to remain with him for whatever reasons, the insights, recommendations, and strategies presented in this book are intended to help you survive and to find some degree of fulfillment in your life because you deserve it. You deserve not only to live but also to thrive and to have a wonderful life to the degree that such a life is possible with a narcissistic husband.

On the day that you were born, there was much joy. Your whole life lay ahead of you with all of its promises and possibilities. As a child, you dreamed of what you'd do in life and what you'd become. Then, you met him and you were swept off your feet. Somehow though, life hasn't worked out as you thought it would. Somewhere along the way, you lost your dreams and your ideas and perhaps even yourself. You got something you didn't bargain for. Your joy is gone, and you perhaps don't even know why. You might not even be able to explain what's happened to you.

Just go back to your wedding day. He may have said that he'd love, honor, and cherish you, but close your ears and open your eyes and see that the vow he really took that day was to hate, despise, and abuse you until death part you. You have no obligation to remain with him. He defrauded you from the very beginning of your relationship with him.

Since he's perverted his vow to love, honor, and cherish you, you may remain with him or not. Stay or leave. The choice is really up to you. Close your ears to his false pronouncements of loving, honoring, and cherishing and open your eyes to his hatred, his despising, and his abuse. You're the only one who controls your life. The decision of what you do with the rest of your life belongs to you. How will you make that decision?

You've read many stories and heard many voices in the pages of this book, but the final story in this book remains to be written and the final voice in this book remains to be heard. It's your story. How will you write it? It's your voice. What will you say? It's your life. How will you choose to live it? You do have a choice.

Works Cited

American Psychiatric Association. *Diagnostic and Statistical Manual of Mental Disorders*. 4th edition. Washington D.C.: American Psychiatric Association, 2000.

Bach, George R., and Ronald Deutsch. *Stop! You're Driving Me Crazy*. New York: G. P. Putnam's Sons Publishers, 1980.

Brown, Nina W. *Children of the Self-Absorbed: A Grownup's Guide to Getting over Narcissistic Parents*. Oakland, CA: New Harbinger's Publications, Inc., 2001.

Carter, Les. *Enough about You, Let's Talk about Me: How to Recognize and Manage the Narcissists in Your Life*. San Francisco: Jossey-Bass A Wiley Imprint, 2005.

Cloud, Henry, and John Townsend. *Boundaries: When to Say Yes, When to Say No to Take Control of Your Life*. Grand Rapids: Zondervan, 1992.

Donaldson-Pressman, Stephanie, and Robert M. Pressman. *The Narcissistic Family: Diagnosis and Treatment*. San Francisco: Jossey-Bass, 1994.

Engel, Beverly. *The Emotionally Abused Woman: Overcoming Destructive Patterns and Reclaiming Yourself*. New York: Fawcett Books, 1990.

Evans, Patricia. *The Verbally Abusive Relationship: How to Recognize It and How to Respond*. Third Expanded Edition. Avon, MA: Adams Media Corporation, 2010.

Forward, Susan, with Craig Buck. *Toxic Parents: Overcoming Their Hurtful Legacy and Reclaiming Your Life*. New York: Bantam, 2002.

Halgin, Richard P., and Susan Krauss Whitbourne. *Abnormal Psychology: Clinical Perspectives on Psychological Disorders*. 4th ed. Boston: McGraw Hill, 2003.

Instone-Brewer, David. *Divorce and Remarriage in the Bible: The Social and Literary Context*. Grand Rapids: Eerdmans Publishing Company, 2002.

Katherine, Anne. *Boundaries: Where You End and I Begin*. New York: Simon and Schuster, 1993.

_______. *Where to Draw the Line: How to Set Healthy Boundaries Every Day*. New York: Simon and Schuster, 2000.

Kroeger, Catherine Clark, and Nancy Nason-Clark. *No Place for Abuse: Biblical and Practical Resources to Counteract Domestic Violence.* Downers Grove, IL: InterVarsity Press, 2001.

Kroeger, Catherine Clark, and James R. Beck, eds. *Healing the Hurting: Giving Hope and Help to Abused Women.* Grand Rapids: Baker, 1998.

Martin, Troy W. "The TestAbr and the Background of 1 Pet 3,6." *Zeitschrift für die neutestamentliche Wissenschaft und die Kunde der älteren Kirche* 90(1999): 139-146.

Miller, Mary Susan. *No Visible Wounds: Identifying Nonphysical Abuse of Women by their Men.* New York: Fawcett, 1995.

Millon, T., and R. Davis, C. Millon, L. Escovar, and S. Meagher. *Personality Disorders in Modern Life.* New York: Wiley, 2000.

Nason-Clark, Nancy. "The Evangelical Family Is Sacred, but Is It Safe?" Pages 109-125 in *Healing the Hurting: Giving Hope and Help to Abused Women.* Edited by Catherine Clark Kroeger and James R. Beck. Grand Rapids: Baker, 1998.

Twenge, Jean M. *Generation Me: Why Today's Young Americans Are More Confident, Assertive, Entitled—and More Miserable Than Ever Before.* New York: Free Press, 2006.

_______ and W. Keith Campbell. *The Narcissism Epidemic: Living in the Age of Entitlement.* New York: Free Press, 2009.

Vaknin, Sam. *Malignant Self Love: Narcissism Revisited.* Prague & Skopje: Narcissus Publications, 2003.

White, Amy Wildman. "The Silent Killer of Christian Marriages." Pages 99-108 in *Healing the Hurting: Giving Hope and Help to Abused Women.* Edited by Catherine Clark Kroeger and James R. Beck. Grand Rapids: Baker, 1998.